Bonnie L. Catt

12-30-72

SAINTS ALIVE!

THE HUMBLE HEROES OF THE NEW TESTAMENT

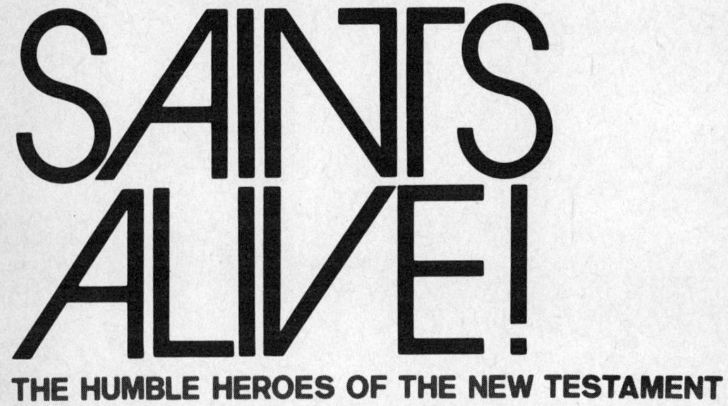

SAINTS ALIVE!

THE HUMBLE HEROES OF THE NEW TESTAMENT

HUBER L. DRUMWRIGHT

Broadman Press / Nashville, Tennessee

4281-16
ISBN: 0-8054-8116-8

Library of Congress Catalog Card Number: 72-79169
Dewey Decimal Classification: 225.92
Printed in the United States of America

To the dear ones with whom I live
All of whom are
in the Lord

Special appreciation to three twentieth-century saints who helped prepare this manuscript: Miss Jane Hill, student at Southwestern Baptist Seminary; Mrs. Richard Bell, pastor's secretary, Southcliff Baptist Church; and Mrs. David Quitty, Southwestern Seminary graduate.

CONTENTS

I WANT TO BE IN THAT NUMBER

ROMANS 1:7*b*

To paraphrase the once popular song, "Did you ever see a saint walking?" In the thinking of many, a saint is some super-Christian who has passed into that celestial dignity on the other side of this life. The last thing many would ever expect to see would be a saint in this world, but in the New Testament world the saints are easily discovered.

The saints in the New Testament are the people of the Lord, all the people of the Lord, not just some. The members of the churches at Rome, Corinth, Jerusalem, Philippi, and Colossae, to mention but a few, are the saints in those places. The Greek word which is translated "saints" suggests dedication, as applied to Christians dedication in the sense of being reserved for God and his service.

In the Old Testament it was the term used to describe the vessels of the Temple that could not be put to common use but were reserved exclusively for the divine service. Likewise, in the New Testament it marked a man as being consecrated to God.

First-century saints, in the Christian sense, were ordinary men and women who were distinguished by one fact alone: they had experienced the saving grace of God in Jesus Christ. Some were working men and would today be called laborers. Some were professional men. Some were wives and mothers. Some were teen-agers. Some were free. A few were rich. Many were poor. Some were slaves. Some were Jews, others were Gentiles. Some were Romans, some Greeks, and some barbarians; but all were saints.

New Testament saints, when known through study of the Scriptures, can reveal much that is of spiritual benefit to those who today belong to God. Peter, John, and Paul, those giants among the saints, were ordinary men, but their spiritual stature sets them apart from common men. Other heroes of the faith also walk across the pages of the New Testament. They are for the most part the unsung infantry in God's mighty army of the faithful, little known men and women who were in the forefront of the action but in the background of the record. But they are there in the record.

Most of the little people of the New Testament, those soldiers in the ranks of the faithful, are not only unknown (even to some Bible students) but their names sound impossibly strange to modern ears. Longfellow insisted that the lives of great men could inspire others to make their lives sublime, but sometimes the lives of great men can be discouraging to the realistic. It can be difficult for the common man to identify with kings, presidents, and generals. The life of an humble man who made good is something else. Some people because they are ordinary people can be an inspiration to others. Perhaps the lives of these humble saints with whom so many can identify will prove a blessing and an inspiration, bringing the understanding that anyone can count for God when his life has truly been offered to God.

The saints on the pages of the New Testament are far from perfect. Perfection is not the hallmark of the saints. Some of them quarrel. Some of them are overly ambitious. Some of them are weak when they ought to be strong. But their very failures and spiritual difficulties can be understood by ordinary men, for such problems are a part of living even in this day. No, it is not an other-worldly quality that distinguished the saints of the New Testament, and because of that their lives can become a warning as well as an inspiration.

When this author was a young serviceman during World War II, he came to the site in the Philippine Islands where eleven missionaries had been executed by the enemy forces who occupied the Island of Panay in December, 1943. As he heard the story of the martyrdom of those twentieth-century saints, he was indelibly impressed with the story of their faithfulness to Christ. After the war was concluded, he discovered, almost by chance, a little poem that had been written by Dr. Francis H. Rose, one of the martyred missionaries. That saint had written:

> All human progress up to God
> Has stained the stairs of time with blood;
> For every gain for Christendom
> Is bought by someone's martyrdom.
>
> For us he poured the crimson cup,
> And bade us take and drink it up.
> Himself he poured to set us free.
> Help us, O Christ, to drink with Thee.

Ten thousand saints come thronging home,
From lion's den and catacomb.
The fire and sword and beasts defied;
For Christ, their King, they gladly died.

With eye of faith we see today
That cross-led column wind its way
Up life's repeated Calvary.
We rise, O Christ, to follow Thee! [1]

Dedication to God has always had its price tag. It did in the first century, and it does in the twentieth century. Martyrdom is not always that price, but the price is always to be paid. There is nothing cheap about the service of God. Once a preacher wrote a businessman asking his support of a worthy cause in the name of Christ. Shortly a curt refusal came which closed with the words: "As far as I can see this business of Christianity is just one continuous give, give, give." The preacher felt impressed to answer the businessman, noting, "I wish to thank you for the best definition of the Christian life that I have yet heard."

The company of the committed is a select company. It is for them that the Savior waits with his "Well done good and faithful servant! . . . You have been faithful in managing small amounts, so I will put you in charge of large amounts. Come on in and share my happiness!" (Matt. 25:23, TEV). My Lord, I want very much to be in that number, when the saints go marching in.

And now, meet some of the saints that will march in that crowd.

NOTES

1. Francis H. Rose, "The Martyr's Hymn," *Masterpieces of Religious Verse* (New York: Harper & Brothers, 1948), p. 413.

BARNABAS:
MR. ENCOURAGER
ACTS 4:36

Barnabas—son of consolation, or of exhortation, or of encouragement. Names were frequently more revealing in biblical times than they are today. Sometimes a name was given to a man because of a particular trait that set him apart from others. Abram became Abraham, father of a multitude. Jacob became Israel, a prince with God. Simon, son of John, was called Peter by our Lord. Peter, meaning "rock," would become "a rock."

Joseph was given a new name by the Jerusalem church. Even today a man may make a name for himself in his church. He may not know his name or be called by it, but he may make a name for himself. Joseph was called Barnabas by his church nearly twenty centuries ago, and therein lies a story.

Joseph became Barnabas because his church felt that the new name especially fitted him. Some translators have understood "Barnabas" to mean "son of consolation." Others have thought it meant "son of prophecy" or "son of exhortation." Unquestionably, the Hebrew language by the prefix "son of" suggests what was judged to be a dominant personality trait. As the book of Acts unfolds, that personality trait of Barnabas becomes increasingly clear. Barnabas was a "son of encouragement" or in today's terms "Mr. Encourager."

Acts gives a thrilling picture of the early church in Jerusalem. This church was especially characterized by oneness of spirit and mutual concern for the well-being of all believers. There were those within the fellowship who were poor and needy, but no one lacked anything because the Christians who owned property, moved by Christian love, sold their property and gave the money to the apostles for the relief of their brethren. Outstanding among those generous-hearted, open-handed believers was Joseph. Joseph, a landowner, seems to have been a man of exceptional resources in the young church. The apostles themselves were so touched by his matchless generosity to his brethren that they began to call him Barnabas, "Mr. Encourager."

Barnabas is not in the forefront of the story of Acts, but he does appear again, this time in connection with Saul of Tarsus. Saul, known later of course as Paul, was destined to become the foremost preacher of Christ. Saul had been chief persecutor of the church at Jerusalem and had actually obtained authority from the high priest to go to Damascus to continue that persecution among the believers there. On the way he was confronted by the living Christ and entered Damascus a changed man. After some time in Damascus, and also it seems in Arabia (Gal. 1:16 f.), Saul went to Jerusalem. This was his first visit there following the great change, his conversion from persecutor to preacher.

Arriving at Jerusalem, Saul was confronted by the unexpected. He couldn't get in the church (Acts 9:26 f.). The church couldn't believe that God could or would reach such a sinner as Saul had been. Could God really reach and dramatically change such a man as that? Reason told the church it couldn't have happened. It must be a trick. Saul must be seeking to infiltrate their fellowship and then betray them all. Incredible as it seems, Saul was held suspect by the church; the disciples there wouldn't accept him.

Only Barnabas discerned the genuiness of Saul's testimony and espoused his cause before the church. How was it that Barnabas was able to discern the genuine ring of this new-found treasure of the Lord, knowing beyond shadow of doubt that Saul was not a counterfeit disciple? The record indicates that Barnabas alone knew about Saul's experience with Jesus on the Damascus Road and of his preaching Christ everywhere. How did Barnabas know these things and the apostles did not? Apparently, he had taken the time and run the risk to know Saul, to hear him out. To the everlasting credit of this encourager of men, Barnabas had the spiritual capacity to discern in the life of another the presence of the same Spirit which he knew in himself to be God's spirit.

What confidence the Jerusalem church must have had in their "Mr. Encourager," accepting the suspected Saul into the fellowship just because of his sponsor! There is a sense in which it was Barnabas who gave Saul to the service of Christ. On the day that he introduced Saul into the fellowship of believers at Jerusalem, he laid at the feet of the apostles a ministry yet to be in the life of Paul, a ministry far more precious than any money that Barnabas had ever brought to his church.

The years passed, but Barnabas and Saul were destined to meet again. Saul had gone from Jerusalem to his home in Tarsus. Those years are silent ones. Practically nothing is known of Saul's work. Perhaps as many as five years passed before Barnabas saw Saul again. Strange news came to the church at Jerusalem. Some believers who had been driven out of Jerusalem by persecution had dared to preach the gospel to Gentiles, and a church made up of Gentiles had come into being in a mighty city to the north, Antioch. The church at Jerusalem was concerned because the admission to the church of Gentiles who had not been circumcised was a critical issue among the brethren. Barnabas was sent as a delegate from Jerusalem to inspect and report on what was actually happening at Antioch.

In Antioch Barnabas found a situation that made him very happy. Gentiles were truly being saved! He knew it was true because he could discern the genuiness of their experience with the Lord. Plunging into that new work with his whole heart, he soon became the leader of it all. Human nature would surely have prompted him to thank God that at last he had found his opportunity for greater service, his larger field. Unbelievably, this encourager of men was thinking about someone else instead of his own success. He remembered Saul. He remembered how the Lord had especially set Saul apart for work with the Gentiles. Saul was the man for this thrilling situation, no doubt about it. Barnabas was not certain where Saul was; he had to go to Tarsus to find him. Find him Barnabas did, and he brought Saul to Antioch. What a day that was for the cause of Christ when Saul of Tarsus and the church at Antioch were brought together, intended by the Lord for one another. It was "Mr. Encourager" who did the job.

Eventually the Antioch church did something that no other church of record had ever done. They sent forth deliberately and prayerfully a missionary party to evangelize Gentiles everywhere it went. Barnabas and Saul carried the responsibility for that work, taking John Mark also with them. On the island of Cyprus where they worked first, things changed. Always Barnabas had been in the forefront with Saul following, but the unusual gifts of Saul brought him into leadership. Saul's name was even changed to Paul, and the two became, significantly, Paul and Barnabas. There is not, however, to be found the slightest hint of jealousy on the part of "Mr. Encourager."

After the return of the two missionaries to Antioch, the Jerusalem Council having indicated their mission to the Gentiles (Acts 15), Paul proposed to Barnabas another tour of the mission fields where Gentile churches had come into being. Barnabas was determined to take with them again his young kinsman, John Mark (Acts 15:37 f.), whom Paul was excluding. A sharp contention between Paul and Barnabas resulted, and sadly it is noted the missionaries were torn apart over that issue.

Paul felt that young John Mark, perhaps in his late teens, had disqualified himself because in Pamphylia on the first missionary venture the young man had gone home. He had turned back and had not remained with the missionary party. Speculation as to the reason for the defection of young Mark has suggested everything from homesickness to resentment of Paul's taking over the work. Whatever the reason, Paul felt it disqualified John Mark from future service, but Barnabas was equally certain that John Mark should go with them. Paul and Barnabas actually split over John Mark, because Barnabas was determined to give him a second chance.

Barnabas took John Mark with him instead of going with Paul. Of Barnabas the book of Acts has nothing more to say. Christian tradition, however, credits John Mark with being the author of "the Gospel according to Mark." Even Paul was later to acknowledge the worth of that teen-ager become a man. Both Colossians and Philemon present Mark as Paul's companion in the missionary work at a much later time. Almost the last words from Paul in the New Testament are: "Bring Mark with you, for he is useful to me in the ministry." In a sense "Mr. Encourager" gave the evangelist Mark to the service of Christ also.

No wonder his church called him "Mr. Encourager," for Barnabas was a man who spent himself encouraging others, especially those in the service of Christ. He stands in the background of the New Testament story, but those he helped certainly came to the forefront in the Christian cause. The ministry of encouraging others, developing their spiritual potential, is open to all believers even today, and the spirit of Barnabas is needed everywhere in the Christian cause. Somebody is just waiting to be encouraged to invest his life for Christ.

PHILIP:
THE GOOD NEWS TELLER
ACTS 21:8

On a summer evening, the boys and girls of our neighborhood all listened for the bells that sounded the approach of the "Good Humor Man." Painted boldly on the side of the truck from which he sold ice cream were the words by which he was known everywhere. Nobody knew his name; he was simply the "Good Humor Man." To a remarkable degree his manner matched those words. He had a friendly smile, he spoke with personal interest, he knew the names of the children. He deserved to be known as the "Good Humor Man."

Philip was called "the evangelist," not in the technical sense of one who conducted revival meetings, but because he was always telling someone the good news of Jesus. Philip the evangelist must not be confused with Philip who was one of Jesus' twelve disciples. Philip, the good news teller came along later during the days of the early church in Jerusalem. He was one of the seven men chosen to help the apostles care for the feeding of the widows (Acts 6:1 f.). Some would have it that those seven men were the first deacons.

Many times God finds his man in the unexpected place, performing the unlikely task. It might be a William Carey mending shoes, a David Livingston working in a mill, or a Philip serving tables for the church. Serving tables was probably no more exalted in the first century than it is in the twentieth, but it was there God found his man for a great task.

Persecution scattered many believers from Jerusalem to many different places, and Philip was one who was driven away. Significantly, he went to Samaria, for Jews had no dealings with the Samaritans. Jesus had said, "You shall be my witnesses in Jerusalem, Judea, Samaria . . ." There it was: "Samaria." If subsequent events are any clue to why Philip went to Samaria, it was in fulfilment of Christ's command to give the gospel to Samaria. Where the Lord wanted the gospel preached, the gospel was not being preached. For Philip that was enough. To Samaria he must go. Others might not care for Samaritans, but Philip did, because of Jesus.

What a revival there was in Samaria! Unexpectedly those mostly unloved people responded to the gospel in large numbers. The entire city of Samaria was shaken; it was truly a city-wide revival. Nothing like it had ever happened before outside of Jerusalem. In fact, when the reports filtered back to the church in Jerusalem, they were heard with grave concern. Could Samaritans really be saved? What did Philip think he was doing anyway? The Jerusalem church decided to send Peter and John to inspect the situation. Interestingly enough, when those apostles got on the scene, they became so involved in the spirit of Philip's work that, though they had said nothing about Jesus to any Samaritan on the way up, they preached in every village of the Samaritans through which they passed on the way back to Jerusalem. There is such a thing as spiritual contagion, and it is a happy day for the church when the leadership catches on to a fuller responsibility for sharing the gospel. Even two apostles caught that from Philip (Acts 8:25).

When things were really happening in Samaria, who would ever have thought that God would have sent such an effective servant to a desert? Many a preacher would have challenged the heavenly computer. "There is more than one Philip around you know. There must have been a mistake. I am the Philip who is doing such great things for God in this important city." There was nothing like that on Philip's part. Out to the desert he went, and he went for one man (Acts 8:26 ff.).

What a man it was for whom Philip was sent, an Ethiopian! In the first century Ethiopia referred to a different territory and different people from those of the Ethiopia of today. Ethiopians today are Semites, but Ethiopians then were Nubians, those black people who today live in the south of Egypt. Furthermore, the man was sexually mutilated, being a eunuch. Jews abhored such a man. Although deeply interested in the religion of Judaism, he could never be a full proselyte, only a "proselyte of the gate," an outsider looking in. He had even been to Jerusalem to worship and was reading the Scriptures when Philip found him, but he was still confused and empty hearted.

Philip was not even fortunate enough to meet his man at the crossroads. He had to run to catch him. The enthusiasm of Philip is directly contrasted with the reluctance of Peter to speak the words of life to Cornelius. Philip was again the good news teller. Sending the new convert on his way, the evangelist went to Azotus and preached all the way up the coast to Caesarea where he made his home through the years that followed.

At home Philip was the same man that he was out before the world. The evidence of this is found in the visit of an overnight guest in Philip's home some twenty years after Philip's arrival in Caesarea.

Paul and his missionary companions were on their way to Jerusalem, returning from a mighty missionary tour among the Gentiles. In fact it was to be Paul's last visit to Jerusalem, for there he was to be arrested and eventually sent to Rome. An almost casual reference to Philip results from Paul's going up to Jerusalem. Coming to Caesarea, the missionary spent the night in Philip's home. The author of Acts designated which Philip it was with the revealing words: "Philip, the evangelist, one of the seven, who had four unmarried daughters that spoke for God."

There is no need to ask if Philip were true to his calling, faithful in telling the good news of Jesus all his days. He had told his own. His daughters loved God and spoke to others the good news even as did their father. Philip did not forget his own. No need to look at a distance for the one who led those daughters to the Savior. Their father stands close at hand.

Inspiration for and commitment to the telling of the good news of Jesus came to those daughters from the same man who believed it was impossible to tell the wrong man about Jesus. Here is the picture of a family reproducing that outstanding characteristic of the faithful father who was known everywhere as the good news teller. "Philip, the evangelist," was an almost casual reference, but the definite article "the" seems to mean much. It testifies to the dominant trait, the consuming occupation of the man. He really was "the good news teller."

PHEBE:
A RADIANT CHRISTIAN
ROMANS 16:1-2

The first century had its own "woman's lib," and Phebe may well be an example of it. She apparently was independent and self-supported, traveling even to Rome to see about matters of concern to her, perhaps even business affairs. More importantly this woman was a Christian, converted out of paganism, as her name indicates. Phebe was one of the names of the moon-goddess known to Romans as Diana.

Phebe was a friend to Paul and also a member of the church at Cenchreae. Cenchreae, only a few miles from Corinth, was the eastern seaport of Corinth. This self-reliant woman, going to Rome on personal business it seems, was apparently intrusted with Paul's letter to the church there.

In the ancient world letters of commendation and introduction were quite common, and even early Christians followed the custom of exchanging such letters when a believer journeyed from his home to a place where he was unknown to the local church. All that is known about Phebe is found in Paul's brief but revealing commendation of her to the church at Rome. Paul commended her to that church, and well he might for she was an inspiring Christian.

Phebe was also identified to the Roman believers as a woman who was a "servant of the church at Cenchrea." "Servant" in Greek was literally "deaconess." Although it was scarcely possible that the term "deaconess" had a technical meaning describing a female officer of the church, it does describe many women of great distinction who faithfully served the cause of Christ in the beginning.

Pliny the Younger, governor of the Roman province of Bithynia, now modern Asia minor, wrote about the year A.D. 112 to the Emperor Trojan about an investigation of Christians. Pliny wrote that it had been necessary to torture two Christian women who were called deaconesses. Another document of the third century mentioned that deaconesses assisted at the baptism of women converts and especially were commissioned to enter heathen homes where there were believing women to encourage their faith, to visit the sick, and to help those in need. Some interpreters have felt that the women mentioned in 1 Timothy 3:11 were deaconesses, but others have supposed that they were the wives of deacons. Phebe was a woman who unselfishly gave herself in the service of Christ after that same manner, being especially inspiring in her character.

Paul indicated to the Romans that Phebe had been his helper especially as well as the helper of many others (KJV reads "succourer of many, and of myself also"). "Helper" or "succourer" was a most significant designation, especially when applied to a woman. Among the Greeks it was a term that described a citizen who took in a stranger to his city, gave that stranger a home, and became responsible for him to the authorities. Phebe was a woman who had in spiritual considerations assumed such a position on behalf of many, even Paul himself. She must have been not only generous in her hospitality toward fellow believers but well respected by her fellow citizens to whom she became an open door for the gospel. She had taken protective charge of the spiritual welfare of many, caring for their needs and interests, as the ancient Roman patron did for his clients.

Now it was the turn of others to help Phebe. Paul asked the Romans to receive her "in the Lord, as becometh saints." It was "in the Lord" that Phebe's claim was presented. Christians did have a claim on one another in the Lord. The Roman believers were to respond to Phebe's needs as appropriate to saints. All believers were saints in those days. As the term suggests, believers were dedicated men, dedicated to Christ and his service. Because of that believers were dedicated to the helping of one another.

In a large mid-western city there lived a woman who never married. She was godly in her life and faithful in her service to Christ. Supporting herself with a small business of her own, she generously supported her church as well. Every cause offered in Christ's name claimed some of her interest. For more than twenty years she was superintendent of a Junior department in the Sunday School of her church. How many of those boys and girls she personally led to the Lord only eternity will reveal. At her funeral grown men testified that she had helped them obtain an education by financial support. A little woman who never had any children of her own had in her own way mothered the many children of others. Her name could well have been Phebe.

Paul was never given to flattery. When he spoke well of Phebe, he meant every word. She was indeed a cherished sister and a devoted friend. She was above all else a servant of Christ. Paul probably wrote Romans while he was at Corinth through a scribe named Tertius, but it was into the hands of Phebe that he entrusted that letter for delivery. Because Paul's commendation of her is placed first in the personal references at the close of Romans (assuming the integrity of the sixteenth chapter) and because it seems to assume the simultaneous arrival of Phebe and the letter, it has been commonly supposed that she bore it to its destination. Renan, the famous French critic of the New Testament, noted that Phebe carried with her in Romans the whole future of Christian theology.

"Phebe" means "the bright one," or "the radiant one." By the grace of God this woman deserved her name for she was truly a radiant Christian.

AQUILA AND PRISCILLA:
A HOME FOR CHRIST

1 CORINTHIANS 16:19

A man and his wife, ordinary people, Aquila and Priscilla were a team for Christ. They were working people, on the go, who seem very modern though they lived long ago in New Testament times. They were city people: Rome, Corinth, Ephesus, great cities had been their homes. They were at Corinth when Paul came there the first time to preach.

Paul met this couple because they were tentmakers as was he. Aquila and Priscilla were displaced persons as well. The emperor Claudius had given an edict driving the Jews from Rome about the middle of the first century. This edict was the result of a disturbance that may have been related to the tension between Christians and unconverted Jews in the synagogues there.

Aquila probably had a Hebrew name also, but this Latin name by which he was always called meant "the eagle." He may have had this name because of a commanding appearance. Priscilla was simply the diminutive of endearment, meaning "dear little Prisca." Perhaps the personalities of this husband and wife were as different as their names would suggest. One thing is certain: they are always together on the pages of the New Testment. In every instance they appear together in their service for Christ, and that service is especially rendered through their home.

The home of those transients must have been modest, but Paul made it his own for almost two years while he was in Corinth. When Paul left Corinth to go to Ephesus, the principal city of Asia, Priscilla and Aquila went with him. Paul wrote to the church at Corinth from Ephesus and included greetings from his fellow workers by saying, "Aquila and Priscilla salute you much in the Lord, with the church that is in their house."

The early churches had no buildings especially constructed for meeting and worship, and were dependent upon the homes of the believers for meeting places. The newly arrived residents in Ephesus, Priscilla and Aquila, must have had a modest dwelling, but it became a center of worship and gospel proclamation. Pastor George Truett often remarked that the foundation of all Christian civilization was the home. Not the church or the school, but the home. He often said that as our homes go, so goes the nation and so go our churches. The churches seldom meet in homes today, for they have their buildings especially designed as a meeting place, but homes and the churches must be one for the good success of Christ's cause.

Apollos was a gifted Jew of Alexandria. He was described as an eloquent man, meaning that he was well educated, and mighty in the Scriptures. He came to Ephesus after Paul had left for Antioch.

Priscilla and Aquila heard Apollos preach. Though he was fervent in spirit, something was missing from Apollos' message. What was missing was difficult to determine. The Scripture says that he knew only the baptism of John, but Priscilla and Aquila helped the situation. When they heard him in the synagogue, they recognized his need, but they did not challenge him nor embarrass him. Instead they "took him unto them," which meant simply that they took the gifted preacher to their home. In their home those humble lay-people expounded to the gifted preacher the way of God more perfectly.

With privacy that would avoid embarrassment, with interest genuine and sincere, the uneducated helped the educated understand more perfectly his ministry. The glowing report which followed of Apollos' work in Greece is no doubt explained in large measure by the help given him in the home of Priscilla and Aquila. Whom to admire the more, the lay people or the preacher, is difficult to know. How admirable were Priscilla and Aquila who knew how to go about helping the preacher! How admirable was the gifted Apollos who was willing to be helped by them. Many a preacher could be helped by many a layman if both were of the spirit of those first century believers, Priscilla and Aquila.

Whoever saw a letter addressed to "Mrs. and Mr."? The man always comes before the woman in the address of a letter. This custom goes back to an earlier day when the order of recognition was even more significant than it is today. In ancient times a man always came before his wife in everything. Interestingly enough sometimes Priscilla is mentioned before Aquila. Paul wrote, "Greet Prisca and Aquila, my fellow workers in Christ Jesus" (Rom. 16:3, RSV). What a testimony this simple fact is to the relationship existing between this husband and wife. It never seemed to occur to Paul, who knew them both so well, that Aquila would be offended by the recognition given his wife. No one seems to have cherished Priscilla more than did Aquila himself.

Very likely this couple returned to Rome from which they had originally been banished, and thus Paul sent them greetings in Romans. At this time he acknowledged that they had risked their lives for him. He also added the observation that all the churches of the Gentiles likewise give thanks for them. What a bold declaration! Could it be that the declaration recalls the fact that two Jews, Priscilla and Aquila, went out of their way to express their own love for converts to Christianity from the Gentile world, whereas some Judaizing Christians seem never to have been able to love the Gentile brethren. Those Judaizers who wanted to fasten upon the Gentile converts all the trappings of Jewish ceremonialism were especially reluctant to have fellowship with Gentile converts around the table or in the home. In fact, it should be remembered that the Gentile church at Rome (or part of it) was meeting in the home of Priscilla and Aquila. Paul added, "Greet also the church in their house" (Rom. 16:5, RSV).

Priscilla and Aquila were ordinary people, but they were used mightily of God. As far as the world would judge, they didn't have very much, but what they had they gave to the service of Christ. They gave a priceless possession when they gave their home. The full contribution of their lives through their home can only be measured in eternity. They gave a home of love and understanding to God's weary preacher Paul. They wisely counseled and greatly strengthened the ministry of the gifted Apollos. They reached out to Gentile converts with the tenderest Christian concern, opening their home time and time again to their brethern for the gathering of the churches. May God give to the world more homes like that of Priscilla and Aquila.

EUODIA AND SYNTYCHE:
A CHURCH FUSS

PHILIPPIANS 4:2

Someone has said that the proof of God's choice of the church is not so much that it is a perfect instrument of his will as that it has survived with as many imperfections as it has. A sensitive Christian is always distressed by the report of trouble in a church. That distress is not relieved by the knowledge that such broken fellowship can be traced back to the churches of the first century.

Beyond a doubt Paul was deeply grieved by the reported trouble in the church at Philippi. He had founded that church and had enjoyed a special comradeship with it through the unfolding years. In fact there is a sense in which it was his favorite church. Then it was reported to him that two of his friends, valued helpers in the work, were seriously at odds with each other.

Paul even named the individuals most involved, though others may have supported the two leaders who had fallen out with each other. Euodia and Syntyche were the two women at fault. By Paul's own pronouncement, these two women were genuine Christians and had helped Paul, Clement, and others very much in doing the work of the Lord. How often it is true that opponents in the church when judged separately are choice people but put together are anything but a spiritual example. Undoubtedly both Euodia and Syntyche were devoted servants of Christ, faithful members of the church, and capable personalities. All the more then was the tragedy of their disagreement which Paul felt keenly.

What could have caused such bitterness between two fine Christian women? Some have supposed they had fallen out over doctrine. In the third chapter of Philippians Paul discussed the doctrine of Christian perfection. All too frequently there has been a breach of fellowship over that very doctrine. Some who have sought the deeper life have given the impression, whether intentionally or unintentionally, that theirs was a superior brand of Christian living. That never makes for very good fellowship. Paul was heard to say on his part: "Not that I have already obtained this or am already perfect; but I press on to make it my own, because Christ Jesus has made me his own. Brethren, I do not consider that I have made it on my own; but one thing I do, forgetting what lies behind and straining forward to what lies ahead, I press on toward the goal of the upward call of God in Christ Jesus" (Phil. 3:12-14, RSV). Following this statement, Paul urged his readers to be thus minded and added, "if in anything you are otherwise minded God will reveal that also to you." "To be otherwise minded" was basically the same term that was used in the admonition later addressed to Euodia and Syntyche that they should be of "the same mind."

Others feel that a more probable explanation of the difficulty between those two women is to be found in the nature of their relationship to each other. Both were energetic women, pouring their full strength into the work. Both were charter members having been with the church from the days of Paul's labor there. Both were leaders, having been associated with Paul and Clement and the others who were definitely in the leadership group. It may have been a first-century situation of "too many centurions and not enough soldiers" comparable to the twentieth century's "too many chiefs and not enough Indians."

Several years ago a seminary class was asked to participate in a survey. Some two hundred people supplied information. The question was asked: "Do you have first-hand information of something in the past which you consider to have been a serious breach of fellowship in a Baptist church that you know well?" The overwhelming majority answered in the affirmative. The second question was, "To the best of your understanding what was the occasion of the trouble?" What a variety of answers was given. Some had to do with the church program: grading the Sunday School, rotating the deacons, building of buildings, and so forth. Some had to do with personalities: the pastor wasn't appreciated for various reasons, members of the church staff were in difficulty with those with whom they worked, and so forth. Some would have been almost amusing if they had not been very serious: should the choir wear robes, should the church house be painted a particular color when it had always been white, should a civic group be allowed to meet on the church premises, etc. It appeared from the survey that the fellowship of Baptist churches was not disturbed by differences over doctrine nearly so much as differences over personal opinions about the practicalities of church life. Some fine Christian leaders would no doubt share Euodia's and Syntyche's embarrassment at being remembered primarily because of their fussing.

Can two strong personalities with different points of view be reconciled? Is it inevitable that these personal clashes occur and worse continue? Paul believed that reconciliation was possible; he believed there was a solution. It was "in the Lord" that hope could be found. Believers were urged by Paul to stand firm "in the Lord." The readers of Philippians were reminded that the Lord was at hand, which probably meant near to their situation. Euodia and Syntyche are also admonished to agree "in the Lord." Each must seek the Lord's will and point of view. By drawing near to the Lord, Euodia and Syntyche would draw near to each other.

A story has long been circulated that tells of a threatened split of one of the Baptist churches in Fort Worth, Texas, during the days that J. B. Gambrell was associated with Southwestern Seminary. The situation was so serious that the two factions in the church could not even agree on any one of the church members to moderate the meeting. Finally, an outsider, J. B. Gambrell was summoned to preside. The congregation gathered; the air was heavy with tension. Before anyone was allowed to speak, Dr. Gambrell called for the pulpit to be moved and in its place was put the large "preacher's chair" that was part of the pulpit furniture. Addressing the congregation, Dr. Gambrell insisted that the Lord was more interested in the well-being of his church than any of its members. He further suggested that the empty chair serve as a reminder that the Lord was present. Each person was to say whatever he had to say as if in the presence of the Lord himself. The meeting by all reports proved to be considerably less difficult than had been expected. To draw near to Christ does bring brethren near to each other.

Someone was addressed by Paul and told to help those women get together. That unnamed someone was called by Paul "true yoke-fellow." Commentators have had a field day trying to identify him. In spite of the masculine adjective some have suggested women. Timothy, Silas, Epaphroditus, and Luke have also been nominated. Some have even suggested that "yoke-fellow" was the name "Syzygus" and never should have been translated into its meaning, but kept in its original spelling like "Euodia" and "Syntyche" were kept though those also could be translated into "Fragrance" and "Affable." Whoever he was Paul felt that the "true yoke-fellow" had the gift of helping heal the wounds and of getting those women together.

What a splendid office it is in the church to make peace! All too frequently even the best of the Lord's servants are given to aggravating difficulties rather than helping to work them out. What an encouragement it is to encounter someone who has the spiritual qualification to help others remember the Lord and find reconciliation in the divine will.

Personal relations in a Christian congregation can be such as to negate its witness. All too frequently even unbelievers are better informed about the trouble in the church than they are about the gospel it proclaims. The consequences of broken fellowship in a church are legion. The blighted witness of quarrelsome churches and the contrasting fruitfulness of a godly fellowship ought to underscore the importance of unity and harmony in the church. Euodia and Syntyche will always serve to recall these truths to the readers of Scripture.

CYRIA:
A CHRISTIAN MOTHER
2 JOHN

The only writing in the New Testament addressed to a woman may well be 2 John. Some believe that "elect lady" in the address of that book was a symbolical term that was descriptive of a church and not a real woman. "Lady," however, was a common name among Greek women, being transliterated into English as "Cyria." In fact "lady" was a common name among peoples other than Greeks, for in Latin the equivalent "Domina" was often used. Among the Hebrews "lady" was the name "Martha."

Often it is noted that in 2 John the pronouns referring to the lady are plural. The inclusion of her children in the thinking of the writer may explain the plural pronouns. The many children that she seems to have had would not be inconsistent with the size of families in ancient times. Some of Cyria's children were young enough to be at home, but others were old enough to have gone out on their own.

In fact the occasion for the brief note that is called 2 John was an encounter between the Christian leader who wrote it, called by the term "elder," and some of Cyria's children who had left their home in the smaller city for the great metropolitan area of Ephesus. It was the even then old story of the young who left their ancestral home for the bright lights and better opportunities of the city.

Cyria was a devout Christian. Her home was the meeting place of the local assembly of Christians. She had implanted her faith in her children also, and her heart must have followed those children who had gone away to the big city to seek their fortune. In Ephesus those children lived with their mother's sister, who was likewise a Christian. The elder, encountering Cyria's young people and being impressed by their faith, did what any parent would understand and appreciate under similar circumstances. He took pen in hand and wrote, "I rejoice greatly to find some of your children following the truth."

It may seem commonplace to note that the meaning of motherhood is found in children, but perhaps this generation needs to hear just that. Just to bring a life into the world does not in itself make a woman a mother. It is the unfolding ministry of a life spending itself in love that gives to the word "mother" that quality which Coleridge expressed in the words, "A mother is a mother still, the loveliest thing alive." Some women have even been mothers to the children of others, with an equal claim on the full meaning of that relationship. Cyria seems to have stood alone in family responsibility. She may have been a widow, or her husband may have been an unbeliever outside the circle of faith. The elder was certain, however, that this mother's heart had followed her children to the big city, prayerfully lifting them up to God, remembering their needs and especially the temptations and trials to which they would be exposed. No wonder that the preacher wrote that his joy might be the mother's joy also.

"To follow the truth" meant to be loyal to the gospel, living in accordance with its demands. Cyria's children were following the truth, keeping the Father's commandments; but this was no surprise for their mother too was devoted to the truth. Christian living is contagious. It is something caught and not just something taught. Many a parent would do well to remember that the communication to his children of his devotion to Christ is of utmost importance. Communication between parent and child does not seem to come easily at any point, but perhaps the greatest failures are registered at the point of communicating faith by precept and example. The young have a greater need of models than they do of critics. Parents teach some kind of religion, even if unintentionally, but there will be no communication of faith except by deliberate design.

A warning was given Cyria to guard her home for the sake of her children. The elder admonished that those whom he called "deceivers" not be received into the house or given any greeting. The elder had asked for love in dealing with fellow Christians, but the love of which he wrote never went contrary to the truth of the gospel. Such love was not to be extended indiscriminately. There were perverters of the truth and enemies of Christ against whom the door was to be closed.

Irenaeus, the early Christian leader, testified that John wrote his Gospel to oppose the heresy of gnosticism as taught by Cerenthus. Gnosticism was a quasi-philosophical approach to the Christian religion. It sought to explain the presence of evil in the world without compromising the character of God. This was accomplished by admitting that the material universe was permeated by evil. God could not, therefore, said the Gnostic, have made the world. Some demi-urge (a subordinate god) was responsible for the creation of the world. The reality of the incarnation of God in Christ was a tremendous problem for the Gnostic. Since matter was evil and human flesh was a part of the material universe, human flesh must also be evil. The Christ, therefore, could not have had an essential union with the human being Jesus. In one way or another for the Gnostic the Christ and the concept of flesh had to be kept separate.

The elder warned against those who would steal away the children of Cyria with their false teaching that Jesus Christ had not come in the flesh. These roving teachers of gnosticism who propagated the heresy that denied the reality of the incarnation did not abide in the doctrine of Christ, which probably meant the teaching of the apostles about Christ. They were the "progressives" of their day. Wandering preachers were given hospitality by believers in the communities to which they came, but in the case of the deceivers who proclaimed heresy, they were not even to be allowed inside the house.

There have always been those who would steal away the faith of the young by their philosophies and pseudo-intellectualism garbed in the finery of progress. Recent years have revealed such strange systems as that represented by the "God is dead" theology of national fame. One of the chief proponents of that heresy was heard to identify himself as a "Christian atheist," whatever that might mean. Most tragically, he was speaking from the platform and lectureship of a Christian university, founded and supported by a major Christian denomination in the United States. Even more tragically there were significant ministers in the city where he spoke who, when interviewed, sounded the refrain, "We must always listen to other people and benefit from what they are trying to tell us." There are times when a Christian has to close the door. It is easy, of course, to react in the opposite direction, finding no one that measures up, because everyone differs from the traditional views held personally. But there is often the unrecognized danger that in the name of openness much spiritual loss comes. Many a parent if he could would have his word with some deceiver who sowed the seeds of skepticism in the hearts of the young, too often in the name of religion.

Cyria was reminded by the elder himself that it was important to love the truth. In fact he assured Cyria and her family that he loved them in the truth. The faithful minister's love was not a sweet sentimentality. It was a love that was rationally and morally conditioned by the gospel. It was the spiritual knowledge of God in Christ that produced that love in his heart. The society of the faithful was established by, and had its very existence from, a relationship to this truth of the gospel. Cyria was blessed, as was her family, by the faithfulness of the Christian minister who wrote to her out of an abiding concern for the spiritual well-being of her family.

SIMEON AND ANNA:
THE SENIOR-CITIZEN SAINTS

LUKE 2:25,36

The elderly woman coming slowly to the front possessed only moderate means; her pension was the principal source of her income. Months before she had fallen and broken her hip. There had been much expense, but she had hoped desperately to make her gift for the Christmas offering. There she came slowly forward with an old fashioned fruit jar in which she had collected her coins, coins collected as she sold the pecans she rose early to gather from the city park near her home. Each morning early before the squirrels got the nuts that had fallen during the night, she painfully made her way from tree to tree in order that she might have money for the Christmas offering. What an inspiration the elderly saints of God can be. Simeon and Anna were two like that.

As the law of the Lord required, Jesus, a firstborn son, was brought by his parents to the Temple when he was about six weeks old to be "presented unto the Lord." The ceremony had double significance. It bespoke purification and dedication. A mother was ceremonially unclean for forty days after giving birth to a child. This strange religious custom was designed originally to remind all of the sinfulness of the human race, a fallen race, and to enter it was to share its problem. The child was caught up in this symbolism also, and thus an offering had to be made, a lamb for the well-to-do and a pigeon for the poorer family (Luke 2:22). Of course, Jesus, the Son of God, was identified with the human family in all of this, not because he shared its sin but because he came to bear its sin.

The law of the Jews since the time of Moses had required also that a firstborn son be presented to the Lord, and Luke apparently combined the rite of purification with the presentation. The presentation was an acknowledgement of God's claim for service on the firstborn son of every Jewish family. Such practice went back in history to Israel's deliverance from Egypt. God had spared, and thus claimed, the firstborn son of every family which had sprinkled the blood of the Passover lamb on its door. From that time on, such sons were ceremonially presented to God for his service. The tribe of Levi, however, was designated as a substitute for the literal carrying out of the requirement of service, and the sacrifice of an animal in the presentation acknowledged that fact. The infant Jesus of the tribe of Judah was thus presented, but there was a deeper meaning of course to his dedication to the service of God. The long-awaited Messiah had come.

Against the background of the ancient ceremonies of purification and presentation, God's senior-citizen saints were introduced by Luke. Simeon was a man who had been promised by the Holy

Spirit that he would not die until he had seen the coming of the Messiah. The impression is given that he was advanced in years, having waited long, and upon seeing the Christ, expressed his willingness then to depart the earthly life.

Much speculation has centered on who Simeon was, for he is not otherwise known in the New Testament. Some have thought that he was the father of the famous teacher, Gamaliel, before whom the apostles appeared (Acts 5:34). All that is certainly known is that he was righteous and devout, looking for the consolation of Israel. The "consolation of Israel" was scriptural language describing the coming of the Messiah (Isa. 40:1; 49:7–10; 51:3; 61:2; 66:13), resulting from his work of comfort.

During the first century the priesthood in Israel was to a large degree involved only in keeping religious regulations and carrying out religious ceremonies, but God had his man of the Spirit ready for that important hour. Being led by the Spirit, Simeon went into the Temple, probably into the court of the women. Finding the infant Jesus, the aged servant of God took the baby in his arms and blessed God. Although the doctors of the law were no doubt in the Temple that day, they did not share in the glorious hour nor did they know the significance of that day. The appropriate high priest was not there to hold the infant Messiah, nor to bless the name of God, but the aged and devout Simeon was God's man for that high hour.

Simeon sang his blessing, called the *Nunc Dimittis* from the Latin translation of its opening words, "Now let depart." This blessing has been in use since the fourth century in western Christianity and the Latin church as a part of the liturgy of evening prayers. Simeon's song especially identified the Messiah with the "Servant Songs" of Isaiah (Isa. 40:3–5; 42:6; 49:6; 52:10). Of undoubted importance to Luke, whose record preserves the song, was

Simeon's emphasis upon the Messiah's meaning for the Gentiles, as well as for Israel.

Following the song, Simeon blessed Joseph and Mary, the infant Messiah's parents. Strangely and prophetically, even in that glad hour it was given to the aged priest to introduce the note of messianic suffering by acknowledging that he would be spoken against and that a sword would pierce Mary's heart because of her child. The shadow of the cross falls across the Gospel of Luke at the very beginning in the words of God's aged servant Simeon.

God had a second witness to validate the appearance of the Messiah. She was Anna, the daughter of Phanuel, of the tribe of Asher. Now Asher was one of the ten "lost" tribes of Israel. The story of the lost tribes goes back to the destruction of the kingdom of Israel over seven hundred years earlier, but some Jews traced their lineage back to those destroyed tribes.

Anna was very old indeed. It is not clear from the Greek text of the New Testament whether she was eighty-four years old or had been a widow for eighty-four years. Even though Jewish girls were often married at fourteen years of age, a widowhood of eighty-four years would certainly mean that she was beyond one hundred years old. Although her age is uncertain, she surely qualifed as a senior-citizen saint. She, too, was led of the Spirit to identify the infant Jesus as the long-awaited Messiah. This woman, who never ceased to worship and never ceased to pray, was chosen by God to be the second witness to the grant event, the presentation of the Messiah in the Temple.

No doubt the priests carried out their routines that day. No doubt all the right words were repeated and all the correct things were done, but they were unaware of the real drama in the Temple that day, the fulfilment of the hope of all the ages. No doubt when aged Anna burst upon the scene and expressed her thanks to God, somebody thought and perhaps said: "There's that crazy old woman again. How odd she is fasting and praying all the time. Wonder what nonsense she is about this time."

Simeon and Anna, God's senior-citizen saints, were like watchmen on the ramparts, looking for the morning of the new day. To their aged eyes of faith it was given to see dawn. The Messiah had come, and they had seen him.

NICODEMUS:
THE NIGHTTIME SAINT
JOHN 3:2

"That's a handsome cat you have," remarked a theology professor from Southwestern seminary. "What's his name?"

The theology student from the same seminary replied, "Nicodemus."

The surprised professor answered, "That's a strange name for a cat."

To which the student quickly replied, "Not so, for he came to us by night."

It will always be that Nicodemus is remembered as the man who came to Jesus by night.

Nicodemus was a common name among both Greeks and Jews in the first century, but only the man who came to Jesus by night bears that name in the New Testament. He was a ruler of the Jews, which might well mean that he was a member of the Sanhedrin, the governing council of the Jews. He was also described by John in his Gospel as a teacher, meaning a religious authority among his people. In fact the Greek text uses a definite article and terms Nicodemus "the" teacher of Israel. He was evidently a preeminent authority on religion in his day.

Some have wanted to protect Nicodemus from any charge of cowardice. It has been suggested that he came not under the cover of night, but because the pressures of the day, the crowds of people who thronged Jesus, and attendant circumstances would have made it difficult if not impossible to have a lengthy conversation on theology at any other time.

Other circumstances, however, seem to reveal a cautious man who was not ready at the moment to be seen, and especially heard, in public with Jesus. As previously indicated, Nicodemus seems destined forever to be remembered as the secret disciple. Nicodemus was again a cautious man as far as Jesus was concerned when he shared in the deliberation of the authorities who were seeking Jesus' arrest (John 7:45–52). He was able only to offer in Jesus' behalf the observation: "Does our law judge a man without first giving him a hearing and learning what he does?"

At the time of Jesus' death Nicodemus entered the story again. Joseph of Arimathea who was a disciple of Jesus claimed the body of Jesus from Pilate. The Scripture notes of Joseph that he acted in secret for fear of the Jews. "Nicodemus also, who had at first come to him by night, came bringing a mixture of myrrh and aloes, about a hundred pound's weight" John noted (19:39). Nicodemus was even then remembered as the man who came by night. He must have been a man of great wealth because he was able to supply such a large amount of spices to be placed between the folds of the linen cloth in which Jesus' body was wrapped before burial; such spices were very expensive.

Nicodemus was a cautious man. When he came to Jesus by night, he revealed that caution even in the way that he addressed the Savior. He called Jesus "Rabbi." Teachers were addressed in those days by three different words, the choice being made on the basis of the feeling of the individual for the importance of the man being addressed. Of those three titles, Rab, Rabbi, and Rabban, Nicodemus chose the middle one.

Nicodemus was a Pharisee, the strictest and the most devout of Jews in observance of the Law of Moses. There was one fact upon which Pharisaic religion rested, and that was the importance and significance of the covenant which God had made with Israel. Nothing was of greater importance to the Pharisees than that they were Abraham's seed. They felt this way, of course, because the covenant had been made by God with Abraham and his seed. The Law of Moses marked out man's part of that covenant relationship. As long as a man was descended from Abraham and kept his part of the bargain by observing the Law, then there followed assurance of God's blessing and favor both for time and for eternity.

When Jesus spoke to Nicodemus, he uttered the memorable words: "Unless one is born anew, he cannot see the kingdom of God" (John 3:3). With these words Jesus was preparing to pull the foundation from under the theology of the teacher of theology. Being descended from Abraham was not enough to bring inclusion in the kingdom of God. There must be a new birth.

There was perhaps a double meaning in John's descriptive term "by night." It was out of the darkness of understanding that Nicodemus asked his questions to Jesus. Jesus rebuked his lack of understanding with the words, "Are you a teacher of Israel, and yet you do not understand this?" In his lack of understanding

Nicodemus represented for John the whole of Pharisaism which was blind to the truth of God (3:19; 9:39–41).

The Jews of Jesus' day were not unfamiliar with the idea of new birth. When a proselyte came into Judaism out of paganism, he was said to be like a newborn child. The mystery religions which were very popular in the first century among the Greeks made the thought of rebirth common even among pagans. The Hermetic Mysteries taught that there could be no salvation without regeneration. The terminology Jesus used was not strange to Nicodemus.

There were two problems with the requirement of new birth as taught by Jesus as far as Nicodemus was concerned. The first was, no doubt, the very idea that such a man as himself needed such an experience. As a devout and pious Pharisee, could he possibly need regeneration? The second question was, perhaps, more sarcastic than foolish, for Nicodemus knew that a man could not enter a second time into his mother's womb to be born again. Nicodemus' second question was not so much "how" as "how for me?"

To Nicodemus Jesus disclosed the fact of the Holy Spirit's work in regeneration, but Nicodemus again pleaded his inability to understand. Jesus had spoken only in simple words, offering an explanation by reference to the wind which, like the Spirit, blows with power across the lives of men. Therefore he rebuked Nicodemus with the observation that earthly things were easier to understand than heavenly. If Nicodemus would balk before even such earthly explanations, he could never deal with spiritual realities.

Nicodemus presents a sad picture of a man struggling with spiritual reality. He probably became a true follower of Jesus as subsequent passages in John's Gospel might suggest, but it is sad that he never openly came out into the light of God's day.

Wealth and privilege, no doubt, stood in the way of discipleship. It wouldn't be easy to give up place and position and the acknowledgement of people to follow Jesus openly. Theological considerations are vital, but there comes a time when a man who only gives himself to the spinning of philosophical and theological ideas finds himself caught in the web of his own making. There is a warning in the life of Nicodemus. It may be possible to discuss the intellectual truth of theology without experiencing the power of regeneration. Christianity is not something to be discussed; it is something to be experienced! The intellectual grasp of truth is important. It is also futile unless it produces a living experience with the power of God's Spirit. Nicodemus at best will always be remembered as the man who came to Jesus by night.

LUKE:
GOD'S EDUCATED SAINT
COLOSSIANS 4:14

Why do we have to spend all this time with theology, all that the people need is Jesus!" The young theological student was expressing his pentup exasperation with his long years of study that day when he exploded in the classroom.

The professor immediately sensing the danger in setting study against witness, as if the two were inimical, hostile to one another, replied straightforwardly but not unkindly: "God may use an ignorant man to serve him, but let us never congratulate ourselves on ignorance, as if we complimented God thereby."

Anti-educationalism often breaks out among God's people, as if the less one knew the more useful he would be to God. Being educated has never been equal to being God's man, but as L. R.

Scarborough of Southwestern Baptist Seminary often remarked, "God seems to have an affinity for a trained mind." Witness Moses and Paul, Calvin and Luther, and on and on the story goes.

To have written almost a third of the New Testament (approximately 28 percent) would be a distinction that would immortalize any man, but it must be added that Luke wrote it uncommonly well. Every evidence points to Luke as the man who wrote the fifty-two chapters that are called *Luke* and *Acts.* This educated man could and did show great facility in the writing of Greek. He wrote the most formal, classical prose in the New Testament and at the same time showed his ability to write in the popular vernacular of his day, the language of the people. Luke wrote only after careful research and intensive investigation.

It is strange for a man who contributed so much to the New Testament to be so little known as a person, but Luke is mentioned only three times in the Scriptures: Colossians 4:14; 2 Timothy 4:11; Philemon 24. From these references it is learned that he was a physician; a faithful missionary companion of Paul, even sharing Paul's imprisonment; and because he is listed in Colossians with Gentiles and not with the Jews, he was most likely a Gentile. That is all that is recorded about him.

There are other possible references to Luke in the New Testament. Once some scholars denied that the name "Luke" (Loukas) came from the Latin "Lucius." Proof that they are the same name has come from inscriptions, in which they have been found interchanged in certain ancient engravings. There are two references to a "Lucius" in the New Testament (Acts 13:1; Rom. 16:21). If these be references to the evangelist Luke, he was a member of the early church at Antioch, came originally from Cyrene, and was later at Rome. It is less than likely that these references to Lucius are to the evangelist Luke. In fact, if they are then Romans 16:21, taken literally, would make Luke kin to Paul himself.

Strangely enough, although much of Acts is written in the first person plural "we," indicating the participation of the author in many of the events described, there is no mention of Luke's name (unless "Lucius" be the same) in that book. Also, significantly, the name of Paul's helper Titus is also missing from Acts. Writing to Corinth, Paul mentioned Titus and then, rather indirectly, said: "With him we are sending the brother who is famous among all the churches for his preaching of the gospel" (2 Cor. 8:18, RSV). Some have thought that the famous unnamed evangelist was Titus' own brother, even Luke. Family modesty is thought then to have been the reason for the absence of both names, Luke and Titus, from the record of Acts.

More certainly God's educated saint can be known through his writings. For instance, he was a musican of no mean ability nor of little appreciation. The angels sing at the Savior's birth, and three hymns of lasting beauty and significance in the church are in Luke's record alone: Mary's Praise of God (the *Magnificat,* 1:46–55), Zacharias' Praise of God (the *Benedictus,* 1:68–79), and Simeon's Song (the *Nunc Dimittis,* 2:29–32).

A late traditon (the sixth century) held that Luke was a painter and that he had painted a picture of Mary, mother of Jesus which was found at Jerusalem and taken to Constantinople. Of course, such a tale is only the product of a pious imagination, but it is mentioned because it was in all probability the literary beauty of Luke's writing, his ability to paint pictures with words, which gave rise to the legend that he had been an artist. The parables of Jesus and the stories in Luke's Gospel were so exquisitely presented that at a very early period they were represented in Christian works of art.

A special characteristic of Luke's Gospel is the prominence that he gave to women. Whereas Matthew's account of the birth of Jesus centered in Joseph, Luke focused the attention on Mary and reveals her heart. Anna, the prophetess, as well as Mary and Martha of Bethany, and the unnamed women of chapters seven and thirteen show something of the prominence of women in Luke's Gospel. Luke also includes two parables of Jesus in which women are the central personages. The first woman's missionary society is identified by Luke, the ladies being named individually. Luke was a man for whom women had been emancipated in Christ.

Luke was a man with compassion for the poor and needy. He records prominently the teachings of Jesus about the danger of riches (12:13–21) and the story of the beggar Lazarus at the richman's gate (16:19–31). When Zacchaeus, the publican, was converted and decided to give half of his goods to the poor (19:1–10), Luke found it worthy of note. Luke sought in every way to relate the teachings of Jesus to the curse of materialism, showing that covetousness was idolatry and the love of money the root of every kind of evil.

Perhaps more significant than anything else about Luke's Gospel, reflecting as it does the author's spirit, is the emphasis given to the universal significance of the Christian faith. Luke shows in his Gospel that Christ is for the whole world. In fact, the book of Acts is noted for its record of the struggle of the early church with the narrow exclusiveness that came out of the Jewish background of Christianity. Christianity's mission is to the whole world, even to the outcast Gentiles. Luke shows Jesus' own concern for outcasts. The lost are especially for Luke's attention (see chapter 15).

Luke was a physician. For a long time it was thought that his writings revealed a medical terminology, reflecting his training which probably took place at Tarsus. Scholars today are convinced that the language of *Luke* and *Acts* was not beyond the competence of any educated, nonmedical Greek of the first century. It should not be forgotten, however, that Luke has always been remembered as a physician. Eusebius, the early church historian, quoted Origen, the most eminent scholar of the early church, as saying that Luke was an Antiochian by descent and a physician by profession. What happened to Luke is not known, but one ancient tradition tells that he lived to the age of seventy-four in Bithynia (some ancient manuscripts say Boetia). He has, however, always been remembered chiefly because he was Paul's physician.

The Methodist church in the small town was filled. People stood around the walls. The windows were open, and crowds surrounded the building, straining to catch something of the service in progress. It was a funeral, but even for that little town which turned out well for such an hour, the crowds were enormous. People had come from all over the county and many from greater distances. He had been a country doctor, the man being memorialized, and had practiced medicine for a lifetime in that one community. Grown men in the congregation bore his name, having been called that name by their mothers who had been lovingly attended by the gentle physician. The elderly had depended upon him. The weather had never been too bad nor the hour too late for that country doctor to answer the call for help. It was commonly said that people owed him more money than he had ever bothered to collect. Somehow when the poor needed medicine, he had always "found" it for them. The young pastor of the Baptist Church in that small town to whom the good old doctor had also given help was asked to assist in the service. Through all the years that have followed, he has remembered lovingly the kind and generous hearted old physician who had helped him and many, many others.

Luke was Paul's physician and will always be remembered for

it. "Luke, the beloved physician . . ." (Col. 4:14). "Only Luke is with me" (2 Tim. 4:11). Some think he became acquainted with Paul in the first place because of ministering to his physical needs at Troas, but whether so or not, Paul always remembered him as "the physician," God's educated saint; and no doubt Paul blessed the name of God for that good man's life and ministry.

NATHANAEL:
WHO TOLD IT LIKE IT WAS
JOHN 1:47

How easy it is to accommodate one's speech to the situation. In fact, by skilful speech, some politicians seem to be able to take both sides of a question, and literally at the same time, talk out of both sides of their mouths. Perhaps all people to some degree or another, face the temptation not to tell it like it really is. Somebody's feelings might be hurt, or it really isn't polite to say what you know people don't really want to hear. To straddle the fence seems at some times to be the only way out. But God had a saint who always told it like it really was, Nathanael by name.

Did a man ever receive a higher compliment than that which Jesus paid Nathanael when he said of him, "Behold, an Israelite indeed, in whom is no guile!" (John 1:47). "Guile" in Greek was the common word for bait, fish bait in particular. Everyone knew what it was to hide a hook in bait for the unwary fish. The word "guile" came to mean "deceit." Jesus said that Nathanael was free from such trickery. Of course, he did not mean that he was sinless but that he was utterly sincere.

Nathanael is not mentioned in the other Gospels, and this seems strange in light of the importance given him in John's Gospel. In the last chapter Nathanael is listed with the seven disciples as a witness of the appearance of the resurrected Christ by Galilee's shore. Attempts, therefore, have been made to identify him with some of the apostles named in the other Gospels. Usually he is identified with Bartholomew because he is never mentioned by John and in the other Gospels he is particularly associated with Philip.

Philip was the one who brought Nathanael to Jesus by declaring that the one of whom Moses and the prophets had written, even the Messiah, was indeed Jesus of Nazareth. Nathanael came, but even as he came, he told it like it really was: he simply couldn't believe that the Messiah would come from Nazareth. It was noted that Cana was Nathanael's home, and because these two communities were close together, it has been said that Nathanael was simply expressing the local prejudice. More likely, it seems that in all honesty Nathanael was revealing his theological views rather than his community feelings. He was skeptical that the Messiah could have such a common origin, could have come from such an insignificant place not even mentioned in the Scriptures of the Old Testament. The common messianic expectation, shared apparently by Nathanael, was that the glory and dignity of the Messiah when he came would be unequaled by any other. Jesus of Nazareth, the son of Joseph, possessed none of those qualities of family, wealth, power, or privilege that would cause anyone to give serious thought to any claim on messiahship.

Nathanael characteristically told it as he saw it, but nevertheless he went to see what could possibly have stirred Philip to such conviction.

When Jesus saw Nathanael coming, he immediately spoke of his outstanding character trait: he told it like it was. Jesus said, "an Israelite indeed, in whom is no guile." Nathanael was not one to be taken in by a ready compliment. Characteristically he challenged Jesus with the words, "How do you know me?"

A strange explanation followed: "Before Philip called you, when you were under the fig tree, I saw you."

Upon that simple answer there followed the most remarkable and unexpected response from the man who always told it like it was: "Rabbi, you are the Son of God! You are the King of Israel!"

Such an immediate and full response to Jesus by the utterly sincere Nathanael needs an explanation. Fig and olive trees, as well as grape arbors, provided rabbis with suitable places for meditation, prayer, and even teaching of the law. There is some evidence that "being under the fig tree" had even become a figure of speech in the first century, indicating a time of prayer and communion with God. In the western part of the United States a hundred years ago it could have been said of the preacher that he "was in his closet" in a house that had no closets. "In his closet" meant that he was keeping the scriptural admonition: "But thou, when thou prayest, enter into thy closet, and when thou hast shut thy door, pray to thy Father, which is in secret" (Matt. 6:6). Even so to be "under the fig tree" probably meant to be alone with God in prayer.

Jesus must have given Nathanael reason to believe that he had known of the prayer which he had made even before Philip came. Perhaps Nathanael had been praying even in connection with his hope that the Messiah would soon come. Philip's ready appearance with such a message and then Jesus' words indicating that he had knowledge of Nathanael's very prayer to God would have been enough to overwhelm him and bring such an acknowledgement: "Rabbi, you are the Son of God! You are the King of Israel!"

That Jesus called Nathanael an Israelite without guile may be an additional play on words, for Jacob, the original Israelite, had been anything but a man without guile. Then there came a day when he, too, was confronted with the reality of God's presence. When Jacob left Beersheba for Haran, he came at the end of a day to a likely camping place and made a bed for himself with a stone for a pillow. During the night, he dreamed of a ladder set upon the earth; the top of which reached to heaven. He saw angels of God ascending and descending on it. Then the Lord himself stood above it and said: "I am the Lord, the God of Abraham your father . . ." (Gen. 28:13*a*, RSV). When Jacob arose from his sleep, he said: "Surely the Lord is in this place; and I did not know it" (Gen. 28:16, RSV). That very place became to him the house of God, the gate of heaven.

It seems most likely that Jesus had Jacob's experience at Bethel in mind when he said to Nathanael "Truly, truly, I say to you, you will see . . . the angels of God ascending and descending upon the Son of man" (John 1:51, RSV). Nathanael was a real Israelite at heart, not just in outward appearance. He, too, had come to acknowledge the presence of God, this time in the person of God's Son, Jesus the Messiah.

Beyond any doubt, Nathanael in John's Gospel is representative of the pious, God-fearing Israel that finds its completion and prophetic fulfilment in the acceptance of Jesus of Nazareth as the Messiah. More importantly, Nathanael is evidence and proof of that which resides in Jesus himself. As John later says of Jesus: "But Jesus did not trust himself to them, because he knew all men and needed no one to bear witness of man; for he himself knew what was in man" (John 2:24–25, RSV). Nathanael further represents the kind of man to whom Jesus can trust himself.

"Jesus saw Nathanael coming to him, and said of him, "Behold, an Israelite indeed, in whom is no guile!" (John 1:47, RSV).

THEOPHILUS:
THE UNKNOWN SAINT
LUKE 1:3; ACTS 1:1

On the tomb of the Unknown Soldier in Arlington Cemetery are the words "known only to God." Across the books of Luke and Acts in the New Testament there must be written after the name of Theophilus, to whom those books were addressed, the words "known only to God." Theophilus to whom almost one-third of the New Testament was written is truly the "unknown saint."

Some have thought that he never even existed, for the name Theophilus is translated either "friend of God" or "lover of God," and so some have considered the name to be only a symbol of any person of that character or description. Thus "Theophilus" should be considered as nothing more than a literary device, in imitation of contemporary writings, which was designed to secure a wide use of Luke and Acts according to such persons.

To the contrary it should be noted that dedications for literary works such as Luke made to Theophilus were quite common in ancient times. Cicero, the Roman poet, dedicated his *De natura Deorum* to Brutus and his *De senectute* to his close friend Atticus. Seneca, the Roman philosopher of interest to students of the New Testament because of his brother Gallio before whom Paul was tried in Corinth, dedicated his *De vita beata* to that brother.

Theophilus was given by Luke the title "most excellent," which was a lofty designation of a Roman officer of equestrian rank, originally a Roman knight." Paul addressed the Governor Festus with this title (Acts 26:25), and Tertullus whom the Jews had hired to prosecute Paul also gave this title to the Governor Felix. Zahn, the New Testament scholar, noted that there is a difference between the address "most excellent" in Luke 1:4 and the simple "O Theophilus" of Acts 1:1. He felt because of that difference that Theophilus was not a disciple when addressed as "most excellent" because early Christians did not use such titles for one another. The absence of the title in the address of Acts was thought to mean that Theophilus had become a Christian before the writing of that part of Luke's work.

In all likelihood Theophilus was a real man, an important Roman officer who had either become a Christian or was deeply interested in Christianity. William Ramsay felt that "Theophilus" was a most unlikely name for a Roman officer in the first century so he concluded that it must have been a name given him at his baptism, as it was customary for people coming out of paganism to take Christian names at the time of their baptism. Because there is no trace of the use of baptismal names in the narrative of Acts, Ramsay concluded that the use of this private, Christian name in the dedication further suggested that at the time of the writing of

Luke and Acts it was dangerous for a Roman of rank to be recognized as a Christian.

Tacitus, the Roman historian, told in his *Annals* that Christians who were detested for their outrageous practices were blamed by Nero for the fire which destroyed Rome on the night of July 18, A.D. 64. To divert suspicion from himself, the Emperor blamed the Christians, and in Rome a grim persecution followed which eventually led to Christianity's being outlawed throughout the empire. After Nero's persecution, Christians were in a most difficult position, because they were counted as followers of an illegal religion. There were none for whom this was more serious than for Roman converts such as Theophilus.

Paul was likely executed by Nero in A.D. 67 or 68. Some believe that Luke and Acts were written in order to provide a defense for the apostle before the Roman authorities to whom he had appealed. It does seem abundantly evident that Luke took great interest in showing that Christianity was not subversive and that a man could be a loyal Roman citizen and also a Christian.

Christianity had originated within Judaism, but the Jews were an unloved race in the Roman world. In A.D. 49 the Emperor Claudius had banished all the Jews from Rome. In A.D. 66 a pogrom broke out in Alexandria which brought death to more than fifty thousand Jews. Time and again the Jews were persecuted across the empire. The climax came in A.D. 70 with the Jewish war of rebellion. Jerusalem was eventually captured. The Temple was destroyed, and the Jews everywhere were banded as traitors.

Was Christianity to fall with Judaism? Was it impossible for a Christian to be a loyal citizen of Rome. Luke wrote to show that Christ and the disciples were pronounced innocent of any crimes by Roman authorities. He wrote to show that Christians were not revolutionaries, Christ himself having turned his back on political revolution. Christians were not barbarous men, given to all vile superstitions as most Romans thought, but were indeed men of decency and dignity.

To produce a book was even more expensive in ancient times than it is today. Usually some wealthy benefactor underwrote the expense of the publication. Under such circumstances it was customary to dedicate the book to the man whose money made it possible. Some have considered Theophilus to have been Luke's patron after this fashion, providing the expenses for the publication and circulation of his work, and thus the dedication was made.

B. H. Streeter authored the idea that Theophilus was the secret name among the Christians for Titus Flavius Clemens, a cousin to the Emperor Domitian himself, and held by some to have been the heir-presumptive to the imperial dignity. It is known that this highly placed man had a wife Domitilla who was either a Christian or strongly sympathetic to Christianity. Her husband might well have been attracted to, or had an interest in, the Christian faith. Domitian put his cousin, Flavius Clemens, to death and had Domitilla banished on the grounds of "sacrilege." Eusebius, the early church historian, says that Domitilla and many others were exiled to the island of Pontia in the fifteenth year of Domitian (A.D. 95) because they were Christians.

To most Christians today to be a friend to God has never been put within the context of persecution and martyrdom. Not many have faced the choice of the gospel or the government. The Christians of the first century ultimately knew that choice well. Christians of other centuries have also known the price that was required by governments when a man was thought to be God's friend. Theophilus may very well have paid with his life to have his name in God's book, but the gospel he embraced brought down the government that persecuted God's friends.

When Bishop Ridley and Bishop Latimer were burned at the stake on October 17, 1555, at Oxford, England, Latimer spoke his memorable words to Ridley: "Be of good cheer, Ridley; and play the man. We shall this day, by God's grace, light up such a candle in England, as I trust will never be put out." No one remembers who Latimer and Ridley were, but men like those changed their land. No one knows who Theophilus was, but men such as he have changed their world.

EPAPHRAS:
CHRIST'S SLAVE
COLOSSIANS 1:7

We demand our rights!" The angry young man standing on the raised stonework surrounding the university quandrangle shouted through the amplifier. The crowds were gathered before the public building with placards which in one way or another read, "Give us our rights." The marchers shoved, and the police shoved back to keep them from entering the national political convention where they intended to demand their rights. The spirit of the times is to demand one's rights, and "slave" is a designation that no one would allow another to put upon him and certainly not claim for himself.

It is remarkable that Epaphras was called "Christ's slave," even in the first century. Sixty million miserable human beings were slaves in the Roman empire in Paul's day. Some were more fortunate than others. Some were even in the imperial household, but no one voluntarily gave himself to slavery. Slaves had no rights. They were at the mercy of their owners. Beyond the imagination of modern men who have never known a single slave were the hopelessness, heartache, and suffering that was attendant upon slavery in Paul's day.

It is remarkable, indeed, that Epaphras was called "Christ's slave," for though Paul frequently referred to himself in this fashion, he refrains from designating others in this manner. Epaphras and Timothy are the only exceptions. Again and again Paul called himself "Christ's slave" (most often translated "servant"), and it is all the more remarkable that he shared it with very few. When Paul thought of himself as a slave of Christ, he undoubtedly was thinking of his total commitment to Christ to whom he owed everything. His will had become Christ's will. His way had become Christ's way. He was totally dependent upon the mercy of Christ. Especially he thought of man who was unusually devoted to the service of Christ after this manner. Epaphras must have been a man completely devoted to Christ's service, claiming no right as his own.

The name "Epaphras" was common in New Testament times, being a shortened form of "Epaphroditus," after the same fashion that people today shorten "Thomas" to "Tom." Epaphras came from the city of Colossae in Asia and from the church that is chiefly remembered because of the letter Paul wrote to it, Colossians. Epaphras of Colossae should not be confused with Epaphroditus of Philippi, another of Paul's friends by the same name. Whereas today Epaphroditus of Philippi would be called a layman, Epaphras of Colossae would now be called a pastor.

Epaphras seems to have been a missionary-evangelist who had

been the first to bring the gospel to an entire district in the Roman province of Asia (Col. 4:13). Ancient tradition not only lists him as the bishop of Colossae but notes that he suffered martyrdom for Christ in that place. Quite possibly, he had been the founder also of the churches at Laodicea and Hierapolis, neighboring towns to Colossae in the Lycus river valley.

Although Paul never personally ministered at Colossae, Epaphras seems to have been one of his converts. It may be that Epaphras was in Ephesus while Paul was in that other great city of Asia. In fact Acts 19:10 tells of all in Asia hearing the word of the Lord at that time.

The Christians at Colossae learned of Paul's imprisonment, and Epaphras went to him to give support in that time of need. It does seem strange, however, that it was the pastor who went on such a mission rather than one of the laymen such as the church at Philippi had sent. An explanation may be found in the situation at Colossae. Trouble was brewing. Heresy was on the horizon. Perhaps Epaphras was anxious to go to Paul himself in order to consult with him about that difficulty. It was out of that consultation that the matchless epistle Colossians was written and sent back to the church, seeking to crush the error that was gaining headway. One of the grandest of all Christological pronouncements Paul made in his letter to the church in the relatively unimportant town of Colossae.

Some have wondered why Epaphras did not return with the letter to his church. Tychicus, instead of Epaphras, was Paul's messenger that carried Colossians. Although nothing can be proved, the epistle which Paul wrote to Philemon, who lived in the same town, which was sent at the same time may contain the answer. To Philemon Paul described Epaphras as a "fellow prisoner in Jesus Christ." In Colossians Paul used the same terms to describe Aristarchus as his fellow prisoner and described Epaphras, whom he also mentioned in that letter, as his fellow servant. Looking back at Philemon, it is discovered that the terminology is reserved, and Aristarchus is described as Paul's fellow worker. This exchange of terms has given the impression to some that the companions of Paul took turns sharing his confinement in order to serve him, the newly arrived Epaphras replacing perhaps Tychicus. If "fellow prisoner" be taken literally, it would mean that Epaphras had been arrested himself because of his association with Paul and was thus prevented from returning to Colossae with Paul's messages.

Epaphras, the faithful pastor, was burdened for his people at home. Paul wrote of him that he always prayed for the home church, especially that the brethren might be "mature and full assured of the will of God" (Col. 4:12, RSV). "The will of God" is a significant phrase. Those who stirred up heresy at Colossae were following their own will, proclaiming human philosophies. Epaphras, Christ's slave, had no will of his own. His will was captive to God's will. He coveted for his people the dedication and devotion to the will of God which had become meaningful in his own life.

All that is known of the Colossian heresy which gravely concerned Epaphras and which prompted Paul to write Colossians is contained in that epistle itself. The heresy was an attack on the total adequacy and unique supremacy of Jesus Christ. The heretics believed that God could not come in human flesh to help mankind but must gradually, through a long line of intermediaries, make his approach to man, each one a little less close to God and yet at the same time a little nearer to mankind. Jesus was just the last and least divine of that long line. This concept of the heretics probably opened up the worship of angels, which Colossians condemned, as well as a strange, occult astrology. Because of this, Paul set out the matchless claims for Jesus as the image of the invisible God (1:15), the very fulness of the Godhead in bodily form (2:9), which distinguish Colossians as of utmost importance to the Christology of the New Testament. When the letter was finished, Paul had declared that Jesus in his person and work was the heart of all doctrine. He declared Jesus the preexistent Son of God to have been the divine agent in the creation of all things, sustaining and operating the whole universe as well, the exalted redeemer and head of the church. A pastor like Epaphras who belonged wholeheartedly to Christ could not have tolerated the heresy against which Paul inveighed. Any doctrine that made Christ less than supreme Lord would immediately be known as heresy to a man who was Christ's very own slave.

Epaphras, the pastor, agonized in prayer for the church back home that his people might stand firm and immovable in the will of God. Strange as it may seem, a man like Epaphras would readily embrace the most hated and despised word in the language, a slave, as his own glory. It was to him a "sweet savor unto life," this being always led in the triumphal train of Jesus Christ as his slave. At the very center of Christian proclamation is the truth that by losing his life to Christ a Christian finds real life.

EPAPHRODITUS:
A CHRISTIAN SOLDIER
PHILIPPIANS 2:25

On Thursday, April 8, 1965, with the arrest of fifty-two Baptist laymen and pastors, half of the churches of western Cuba were left without leadership. The next Sunday, however, not a single church failed to have its regular worship service. Laymen, Sunday School teachers, deacons, and in two instances, the wife of the arrested pastors stood before the people of God to speak with boldness the gospel of Christ. Those people did not know what would happen to them for leading public worship in Baptist churches, but they were all willing to pay whatever personal price was necessary for the gospel to be proclaimed. Several of the churches remained for several months without pastoral leadership, and one of the larger churches waited three and a half years for the return of its pastor from prison. During those months and years the laymen carried the responsibility of leadership in the churches.

Epaphroditus of Philippi was a Christian layman sent by his church to help Paul during his imprisonment in Rome. The church that sent him was especially dear to the imprisoned preacher and had frequently been a source of material and spiritual support for him. When the church at Philippi learned of Paul's difficulty at Rome, it responded quickly to send Epaphroditus to his assistance, to minister to his needs. Paul needed money for his defense and also, no doubt, to pay his living expenses, if he were to live under guard outside the terrible Mamertine prison. More than money, however, Paul needed friends and their love. Epaphroditus did more than bring a gift of money. He gave himself to Paul as well. No wonder Paul described him as "my brother, and companion in labor, and fellow soldier." It seems that this description marches on in ascending order, reaching its climax in "fellow soldier."

Christian brotherhood is a miracle and always has been. Think of the dissimilarity between Paul and this man whom he called "brother." One was a Jew and the other a Gentile. In the ordinary channels of human life twenty centuries have not been able to erase the difference between Jew and Gentile, a difference attended by fear, hatred, and even violence. "Epaphroditus" was a Greek name meaning "dedicated to Aphrodite" who was a pagan goddess known as Venus among the Romans. The love of Christ had bridged that great gulf and two men greatly different in background and upbringing were bound together in the tender tie of brotherhood. The glory of Christian brotherhood has often been tarnished by the shoddy lives of those professing Christ, but when men have offered themselves to one another as brothers in the name of Christ, nothing has shown more brightly, crediting the gospel in the eyes of men with great good.

Epaphroditus was also Paul's companion in labor. Just exactly what befell him in Rome is unknown, but he nearly died. His sickness was in some way related to his work for Christ (Phil. 2:30). Some have supposed that the layman from Philippi fell victim to one of the fevers that frequently spread like fire through the congested city of Rome. Others have concluded that he suffered physically, being persecuted and abused because of his association with Paul the prisoner. It may be that illness had come because of his devoted service to Paul; he may have worn himself out in personal ministry to the preacher. All that a great distance prevented the Philippian church from doing for its beloved founder, its delegate no doubt sought to do. He seems to have served as Paul's personal servant and attendant in that time of special need.

War had been declared! God was at war with the wickedness of this world and Paul was leading the troops. Epaphroditus unhesitatingly enlisted, throwing himself into the battle. Paul called him his fellow soldier.

In his writings Paul seems especially fond of representing the Christian life as a spiritual warfare. He wrote to Timothy and admonished him to "endure hardness, as a good soldier of Jesus Christ" (2 Tim. 2:3). He wrote to encourage the Ephesian believers to put on "the whole armor of God" (Eph. 6:13). When the mighty servant of Christ summarized his own life, he said "I have fought a good fight" (2 Tim. 4:7). Bishop Lightfoot has concluded that the spiritual trilogy "brother, companion, and soldier" indicated that the layman was one with the preacher in sympathy, work, and risk.

Two other insights are given into the life and service of Epaphroditus, God's layman soldier. He is spoken of as the "messenger" of the church at Philippi. "Messenger" is "apostolos" in Greek from which the English word "apostle" is transliterated. In early Chrisitianity it came to have the loftiest significance. In itself it simply meant that one was sent with a message. Because it referred to one under such instructions, it became the term with which those were designated to whom Jesus personally instrusted the gospel. Paul would highly honor Epaphroditus by taking such a word to describe him. It must have seemed appropriate to Paul because the good layman was a man under orders to discharge a sacred trust and as a good soldier, he was carrying out his orders.

George Truett often quoted the poet and said that duty was the sublimest word in the English language. No man owes a higher duty than that which he owes to the service of Christ, and when he meets the responsibility well, he is a good soldier of Jesus Christ.

Paul also said that Epaphroditus had ministered to his wants. The term "ministered" is a verb, but the noun from that same root is translated "servant." It was truly a magnificent word in secular Greek, and Epaphroditus was a Greek. When Greek city-states thrived, "servant" (*leitourgos*) was used to designate a citizen who, because he loved his home devotedly, undertook heavy, and often expensive, public obligations. Sometimes he underwrote the expenses of an ambassador who was sent to open contacts or make peace with other states. Sometimes he financed the writings of a drama, which the Greeks greatly enjoyed, to be given freely to the public. Sometimes he provided for the training of athletes who would represent his city in the games, very much as some today make contributions for the Olympic contest. Sometimes when danger threatened he paid for the equipping of a warship to protect his city. Nearly always, the "servant" was one who unselfishly, out of great love and much personal cost, gave himself to others. This was the word that Paul applied to the good layman Epaphroditus.

There always has been and there always will be a personal cost to the individual whose life counts for Christ. Such is gain, not loss, but it is cost nonetheless. Paul said that Epaphroditus didn't even regard his own life. Stated positively, he hazarded his life. Actually, it pictures a gambler in ancient times who risked a prize on the turn of the dice. Epaphroditus risked his life for Christ; he staked everything on his Lord. When everything has been said and done, the ultimate measure of a soldier's faithfulness has been the risking of his life itself. In the spiritual warfare surrounding the Christian, the command is still, "Be faithful to death." Christ is worthy of our very lives, or he isn't worthy at all.

ONESIPHOROUS: *A BREATH OF FRESH AIR*

2 TIMOTHY 1:16

Names of people once had special meaning. A moment's reflection tells the story of the Bakers, Taylors, Smiths and many others, simply by the meaning of the name. Names may not have special meaning in modern times, but they did in New Testament times. It was strange how often a man then lived up to his name. The Jews named their children hoping it would be like that, and even the pagans had aspirations for their children expressed in the names given them. Often the transforming power of Christ took a man's life to the fullest realization of such dreams.

Onesiphorus may sound strange in the ears of twentieth-century Americans, but it sounded wonderful to Paul in the prison cell at Rome where he awaited execution. Onesiphorus is Greek, and it means "refresher" or "bringer of benefit." As far as Paul was concerned, this Christian convert from paganism certainly lived up to his name. All that is known of him is found in 2 Timothy 1:16–18.

Onesiphorus was a member of the church in the great city of Ephesus, and he loved Paul devotedly. When the layman came to Rome, for reasons that are not disclosed in the Scriptures, it is said that he sought very diligently to find Paul. Tradition says that Paul was in the Tullianum, or dungeon, of the loathsome Mamertine prison. To locate Paul and have access to him under such circumstances would indeed have been difficult. Though such a location for his imprisonment has been questioned, it seems that Paul was under a much more severe military custody than anything he had known in earlier imprisonments.

How much the coming of Onesiphorus meant to Paul! In 2 Timothy 1:15 Paul indicates that all his friends from Asia had turned away from him in the hour of his supreme agony. It was just then that Onesiphorus found him. Only imagination can reveal the difficulties encountered by this stranger in Rome as he sought to find Caesar's prisoners, but to his everlasting credit, he found Paul. Persecution was in the air. Nero had inaugurated it, having blamed Christians for the burning of Rome in July of A.D. 64. To get involved with Paul was almost to throw one's life away at a time like that; no wonder the folks from Asia went home.

Some people make very little contribution to the lives of others. Even some Christians make very little contribution to the lives of other Christians, especially if there is any personal cost attached. Some people think only of themselves and approach life with self-interest only, willing to receive but unwilling to give. Few people really make an investment of themselves in others. Even in this day, few are willing to become spiritually involved with the needs of others. Few people seem to be concerned about someone else.

Onesiphorus was like his Master in that he did not spare himself. Paul said that he was often refreshed by him. He was a spiritual tonic for Paul. That Paul, the mighty man of God, would have needs is not easy to remember, but he did. Moffatt came to the heart of it when he translated Paul's words about Onesiphorus, "he braced me up." The layman helped the preacher to face the huge demands of his service to Christ.

Occasionally, an indiviual will rise above his ordinary level of living to respond dramatically to the need of a crisis time. This was such a crisis time for Paul, and Paul was certainly a man to inspire other men to noble deeds and sacrificial living. Onesiphorus would have been worthy of commendation if these things alone had been true, but he is even more worthy because Paul reveals such response to have been the settled practice of his Christian life. The King James' Version gives Paul's words as: "and in how many things he ministered unto me at Ephesus, thou knowest very well" (2 Tim. 1:18*b*). The best manuscripts of the Greek text, however, omit the phrase "unto me." What Onesiphorus had done in Rome he had also done at home in Ephesus. What he had done for Paul he had also done for others, perhaps for many. So wide and inclusive was Onesiphorus' involvement with people that Paul was simply able to say to Timothy "you know all about what kind of person he is."

Selfishness, or personal concern, keeps Christians from a meaningful involvement with others, their Christian brethren and the entire human family as well. The price of involvement is high. It is paid nearly always in something other than money. The price is always in terms of self and the intangibles of human life. Paul said that Onesiphorus "was not ashamed of my chain." At a time of crisis and terror when others were turning away, not only because of fear for their own lives but also because Paul was branded as a criminal, Onesiphorus was not ashamed of his association with him. All the shame and disgrace that could even turn away close friends are concentrated in that one phrase "my chain." Many a Christian has been turned from the path of duty and witness by the mocking laughter of an associate or the ridicule of a crowd. The pressure of social disapproval is as real today as it ever was. For that stalwart Christian from Ephesus, there was to be no weakening of resolution, no withdrawing from the situation of need. If anything, the sight of Paul in chains broke his heart and melted his life into the fluidity of service.

Because Paul, in his acknowledgement of his friend, invoked a blessing only upon the house of Onesiphorus and not on the man also, some have supposed that the good layman had already lost his life. Paul asked that Onesiphorus might find "mercy from the Lord on that Day." This statement has been further cited to support the belief that death had already taken the preacher's friend. In fact, a certain church has cited this reference as an example of prayer for the dead.

A single explanation of Paul's interest in Onesiphorus is both plausible and likely. At a time when all from Asia were turning away, the house of Onesiphorus of Ephesus in that very province of Asia was different. Why did Onesiphorus come to Rome? Could it be that when word of Paul's situation came back to Ephesus in Asia the family of Onesiphorus sent him to Rome or at least gladly cooperated with his going for the very purpose of making up the deficiency created by the departing Asians? This would be reason enough for singling out the man's family for a blessing.

As far as the appeal for mercy for Onesiphorus, "On that Day," is concerned, Matthew 25:31–40 would justify the prayer. As Matthew gives the record, Jesus said that in the day of his glory and judgment the King would say to those on his right hand: "come ye blessed of my Father, inherit the kingdom prepared for you . . . for I was in prison and ye came unto me." Then the righteous shall answer and say, "Lord when saw we thee . . . in prison and came unto me." Onesiphorus and others like him will find some mercy on that day.

TITUS:
GOD'S MAN FOR ALL SEASONS
2 CORINTHIANS 2:13

Great men must be viewed against the background of their times. Lincoln, the emancipator, is forever identified with the crisis that rent this nation a little more than a hundred years ago. George Washington, the father of his country, attained to enduring fame because of the critical and formative time in which he lived. In Christian history men have also been caught up in their times. The deplorable lethargy of organized church life in his day must be remembered when the life of William Carey and the modern missionary movement which he led come under consideration. Although Titus was not in the forefront of early Christianity, he did come upon the scene at a time of momentous importance. A decision had to be made, and Titus is somehow forever linked with the fateful hour through which the early church struggled.

Strangely, this man who was vitally involved in one of the great hours of the early church is unknown by name upon the pages of the book of Acts. There has been much interesting speculation as to the explanation to this fact, because in the writings of Paul himself Titus has such a notable place. In 2 Corinthians when speaking of Titus' relationship to the church at Corinth, Paul notes: "And we have sent with him the brother, whose praise is in the gospel throughout all the churches" (2 Cor. 8:18). Some scholars express the opinion that usage in the Greek language in which the New Testament was written would justify the translation "his brother" instead of "the brother." On the basis of such a translation it is further deduced that Titus' famous brother, mentioned but unnamed in the Corinthian reference, was none other than Luke himself who authored Acts. It is thought that out of family modesty Luke suppressed both his name as well as the name of his brother in Acts. Although such highly speculative conclusions can never be finally supported, it is known through the reference in Galatians 2:3 that Titus was a Greek, even as Luke, and it seems that Paul's reference in the epistle to Titus, 1:4, "mine own son," probably means that Titus was one of the apostle's converts.

Even though Titus is unnamed in Acts, there is one reference in that book that very likely includes him. Equating the experience of Paul as described in Galatians 2 with that described in Acts 15, Titus, the young Greek convert, is included in the "certain other of them" mentioned as going to Jerusalem with the Paul and Barnabas. It is to be recalled that the issue before the Jerusalem conference was of tremendous importance, involving as it did the way of salvation and the content of the missionary message to be proclaimed to the Gentiles. Of all those present, Paul especially considered Titus to have been the test case. The decision by the early church that Titus, who was a Gentile, needed nothing to complete his salvation was based on the evidence of that man himself. Peter declared at that momentous conference: "But we believe that through the grace of the Lord Jesus Christ we shall be saved, even as they" (Acts 15:11). But Titus was "exhibit A" in proof of the position of Paul and Barnabas that salvation came by grace through faith plus nothing. The issue would be decided ultimately by the undeniable evidence of a man's life. Titus, the Gentile who had been saved by grace plus nothing was that man for the hour.

Titus is mentioned more frequently in connection with the Corinthian correspondence of Paul than in any other setting. He was especially valuable in the working out of the problems that existed in the Christian community at Corinth. Some of the scholars believe that Timothy had already attempted to handle the troubled situation in that great city but had failed in the task. Whether this be the case or not, Paul felt that Titus was especially useful in the delicate and demanding situation at Corinth. As a city, Corinth was wealthy, luxurious, immoral, and vicious. This kind of environment created many of the problems that afflicted the church there. The factions that rent the Corinthian church are revealed in 1 Corinthians to have been due not to doctrinal heresies but to the carnality of the believers who were being carried away into sin by their admiration for Greek wisdom and eloquence. What a rock of morality Titus, the Greek convert, must have been to be qualified to deal with the issues of immorality as well as of divided fellowship that plagued the church. Grace was a life demonstration with Titus. Is it an accident that in 2 Corinthians 6 Paul called upon the Corinthian brethren to "come out from among them, and be ye separate . . . and touch not the unclean thing . . . ?" Is it a coincidence that the seventh chapter continued the appeal "let us cleanse ourselves from all filthiness of the flesh and spirit, perfecting holiness in the fear of God?" Paul's grave concern for the Corinthian church is revealed in those statements. With this insight Paul's words are found to be freighted with meaning when he wrote, "But thanks be to God, which put the same earnest care into the heart of Titus for you." Titus was surely God's man to lead the Corinthian church out of the morass of immorality into which it had sunk. His was a living testimony to the life that honored God and proved the reality of salvation by grace through faith.

A book in the New Testament actually bears the name of Titus, written to him by Paul it is believed. From that letter it is known that Titus worked on the island of Crete and led out in the establishment of churches there. Paul, therefore, advised him about the ordination of pastors for those churches. Paul offered his comment about the situation existing among the people of the island in order to guard the quality of men selected: "One of themselves, even a prophet of their own, said, The Cretans are always liars, evil beasts, slow bellies. This witness is true" (1:12–13). Titus was admonished to rebuke the Cretans sharply because: "They profess that they know God; but in works they deny him, being abominable, and disobedient, and unto every good work reprobate" (1:16). In this same letter, however, the apostle insisted that it was not works of righteousness done by men that accomplished salvation. "But according to his mercy he saved us, by the washing of regeneration, and the renewing of the Holy Ghost; which he shed on us abundantly through Jesus Christ our Savior" (3:5–6). Hard upon this pronouncement there followed the admonition: "I will that thou affirm constantly, that they which have believed in God might be careful to maintain good works" (3:8) Titus' affirmation at this point was to be the testimony of his own experience and life. He would be able to make such positive affirmation with entire confidence and be heard by the Cretans because his own life was consistent with the gospel.

How important it was for the man who was preaching salvation by grace through faith to live the life that put good works on display, in the proper place, and with the correct emphasis! Somehow this seems to have been the story of Titus' whole life as a Christian. He was a living proof that salvation by grace through faith was real. No salvation by good works, but it was his life of good works that gave eloquent testimony to the reality of salvation by grace through faith. From the human point of view one could tremble at the thought that Titus might have been an inadequate evidence to saving grace when he was displayed before the Jerusalem council. Suppose that his life had not measured to his profession. What also would have been the fate of the work at Corinth if there had been no man like Titus to send into such corrupt circumstances with both the message and the manner of one who was saved by grace? There could have been no hope for the work in a place like Crete without a man like Titus. The message of Titus' life was clear to every believer anywhere, anytime. It was not only the message which made the man, but the man who made the message. Perhaps it is like that even today: the gospel being validated in every kind of circumstance by the lives of those who have been saved by grace.

SILAS:
THE NUMBER TWO SAINT
ACTS 15:40

To be the number two man has probably never been easy. To play "second fiddle" has never been an enviable role. "Next year I want to start the games; this year I have only been a substitute." The young man who spoke had been an outstanding high school athlete, quarterback of the football team. His first eligible year in college had seen him sitting on the bench most of the time; his second year had seen him playing on the field more often. His dedication to the game and his determination to be number one almost anyone would applaud, but what about the man who must be content with the second place? Especially what about the many who must take the back seat in Christian service?

What did flash through the mind of Silas that day when Paul

asked him to make the second missionary journey as his companion? Silas knew about the bitter separation between Paul and Barnabas. He also knew that the gentle and kind Barnabas had firmly insisted that the young defector, John Mark, be given a second chance in the service of Christ and Paul had hotly rejected the idea. It wasn't easy to work with a man like Paul, who went around claiming to be "the" apostle to the Gentiles and was certain that he was right about everything.

Silas was not by temperment or background a second-place man. Silas is described in Acts 15:22 as being one of the leading men in the church at Jerusalem. Paul probably never thought that he was asking Silas to take the backseat, but Silas, no doubt, perceived that there would be only one chief of the missionary party and it would not be he. The very fact that Silas responded to Paul's invitation (the Scripture says Paul chose him, a note of authority even in the word) was a deliberate act of self-effacement on his part.

Silas is everywhere with Paul, constantly by his side, but not a single word that he ever spoke is recorded on the sacred page. Paul always did the preaching that made the record, not a word from Silas though he was himself a prophet (Acts 15:32). One tradition identified him as having been one of the seventy disciples sent out by Jesus himself. And he had been chosen at the time of the Jerusalem conference to bear, along with Judas Barsabbas, the findings of the brethren to the church at Antioch (Acts 15:22 ff.).

On the second missionary journey, Paul and Silas came to Philippi as a result of the Spirit's leadership. Preaching in the streets, Paul was soon in trouble. A slave girl who was hired out by her owners as a fortune-teller followed Paul and his companions, crying out as she did: "These men are servants of the Most High God, who proclaim to you the way of salvation" (Acts 16:17, RSV). Paul turned and delivered that girl from the strange power that possessed her. Her owners were incensed because her usefulness was destroyed. Paul and Silas were dragged before the magistrates in the marketplace. There seems to have been someone else in their party, for the account has been given with the use of "we," but only Paul and the number two man were arrested. They were both beaten and they were both thrown in jail, the inner prison, their feet being made fast in the stocks. Because of Paul's importance, it is easy to read such an account and forget that his silent partner Silas shared it all, the experience in its fullest.

About midnight, Paul and Silas were praying and singing hymns to God. All the prisoners were listening to those strange sounds. The jail at Philippi had never witnessed a religious service like that. Note is frequently taken of Paul's faith, courage, and devotion that would cause him to sing and rejoice in the Lord at such a time, but remember Silas was there also. He sang and prayed too.

When the earthquake came and cleared a path to liberty for all the prisoners, it was a miracle that no man fled. Would not it have been most likely that even the preacher would have thanked God for such a speedy deliverance and fled the uncertain tomorrow that could bring additional torture, and perhaps even death? Paul remained, even if the stocks be refastened, the door rebarred, and even if again he be beaten. But remember, Silas stayed too.

When the jailer came and saw what appeared to be the empty jail, he would have ended his own life because of the disaster. It was Paul who cried out from the inner darkness: "Do not harm yourself, for we are all here" (Acts 16:28, RSV). The jailer fell down before both Paul and Silas, and he addressed them both: "Sirs, what must I do to be saved?" (Acts 16:30). Silas was by Paul's side in it all, though that is easy to forget.

When Paul boldly refused the anxious request of the magistrates that he leave town without any more attention, he acted, no doubt, out of a desire to see the young church in Philippi vindicated from any charge of wrong doing. "They have beaten us publicly, uncondemned, men who are Roman citizens, and have thrown us into prison; and do they now cast us out secretly? No! Let them come themselves and take us out" (Acts 16:37, RSV). Paul spoke the words as always, but Silas stood by his side in it all. It is further disclosed that Silas, even as Paul, was able to boast himself of Roman citizenship. Silas had his full share in everything.

Silas went on with Paul to Thessalonica and then fled to Beroea with him because of the threatening danger. Somehow, the impression is given, however, that Silas did not excite the personal animosity that Paul gendered, because he was able to stay and encourage the young church at Beroea when Paul was run out of that town and had to leave for Athens. Later, Silas followed Paul on even to Corinth where their association ended as far as the record goes.

While at Corinth, Paul wrote two letters to the church at Thessalonica and in them he mentions having in his company Silvanus and Timothy. There is little doubt that Silas and Silvanus are one and the same person. "Silas" is probably the Aramaic form of the name "Saul," while "Silvanus" was the Latin name used by this Roman citizen because it sounded like his Aramaic name. Because in the postscript to both letters to Thessalonica, Paul changes from the "we" of the main body of the letter to "I" at the close, some have thought that Silas actually contributed to the writing of both letters. If so, he would again be the number two saint, for in common practice both letters are assigned to Paul alone.

The first letter of Peter also mentions a Silvanus as having shared in its production. "By Silvanus, a faithful brother as I regard him, I have written briefly to you" (1 Pet. 5:12, RSV). It would seem again that Silas and Silvanus are one and the same person. Silas must have had considerable literary ability, for the Greek in which Peter's first letter is written is judged to be some of the best in the New Testament. Many believe that Peter was incapable by himself of producing the kind of Greek in that first letter, noting the difference between it and Second Peter as to the literary quality. Silas was an excellent scribe in any way that his work is viewed, either putting Peter's message into Greek or perhaps even assuming much responsibility for the actual arrangement and contents of the letter. As always, Silas was the number two saint, making his contribution by the support of the prominent Christian leader with whom he worked. There is a valued place for the number two man in the service of God.

First Baptist Church of Dallas, Texas, rejoiced for forty-seven years under the gracious leadership of God's incomparable pastor and preacher, George W. Truett. Words could not express the blessing that Truett brought to his people, but there was another man, God's number two saint. Robert H. Coleman for decades stood faithfully and loyally by the great pastor's side. Coleman was a most capable man in his own right, compiling hymnals widely used among Baptists, in many ways making his distinctive contribution. Perhaps most of all, however, he is lovingly remembered because of the matchless contribution which he made to the effectiveness of another man's work for Christ. Like Silas, Brother Bob found God's will in being the number two man.

GAIUS:
WHO HELD THE ROPE
3 JOHN

Some men worship money. A man's money is his life. Energy, talent, ability are all turned into coin. A man really trades himself for money. Other men worship with their money. Gaius was a man who, by means of his money, gave himself to Christian missions.

Three men in the New Testament have the name "Gaius" other than the faithful layman mentioned in 3 John. Some scholars have wanted to identify the Gaius to whom the elder wrote 3 John with one of the men by the same name, all of whom were associated with Paul. Gaius of Corinth was Paul's friend who is remembered because of his hospitality to that great preacher. Gaius of Macedonia had actually been Paul's missionary companion (Acts 19:29) as had also a Gaius, who came from Derbe (Acts 20:4). It seems unlikely that any of these men was the Gaius to whom the elder John wrote.

The Gaius of 3 John would be called a layman today. He probably lived in a small community not far from the great metropolitan area of Ephesus where John, the elder, was the leader of the Christian community. The elder wrote his letter called 3 John because Gaius was in trouble with the leadership of his church.

The story behind 3 John unfolds with a cast of characters. Of course, there was Gaius, the Christian layman who seems to have been turned out of his church by a Diotrophes who was the leader of that church, perhaps the pastor. The trouble between Gaius and Diotrophes was over a third man named Demetrius.

Demetrius during the frontier days of the United States would have been called a circuit-riding preacher. In those beginning days of Christianity, Demetrius was an itinerant evangelist, a wandering preacher who proclaimed the gospel wherever he went. Such preachers, like those that Jesus sent out from among his disciples, took nothing with them but lived from the suppport of those people who heard the gospel sympathetically. Demetrius wasn't the first such preacher that Gaius had helped. In fact, he had a reputation for supporting those itinerant evangelists of whom Demetrius was only one; but he was the cause of the immediate problem.

How was it possible for Gaius to be in trouble with the leader of his church for having helped the missionary? Demetrius had come from the church where John served and was counted as a follower of his, but Diotrophes didn't acknowledge the authority of John, the elder. Apparently, there was a conflict of interest between the two, and it was not to be the last time that one Christian leader would oppose the work of another Christian leader simply because he couldn't control it. It may be that Diotrophes strongly resented Gaius' giving money and help without channeling it through him. If so, it wasn't to be the last time that a church member suffered because he didn't put his money in the hands of someone who thought he had a claim on it.

When the elder, John, learned of the situation, he wrote to Gaius and encouraged the faithful layman. He described Gaius as a follower of the truth. "Following the truth" is particularly Johannine terminology, and it meant that such a man lived the gospel, his life and character being shaped by it, the instruction of Christ being his guide for life. Gaius was commended by the elder, John, for having done wisely the very thing that the "elect lady" of 2 John was warned against doing unwisely: taking into the home the wandering preacher. The elder said that Gaius had done well "to bring forward on their journey" those proclaimers of the gospel. Such an expression in the New Testament (Acts 15:3; 20:38; 21:5, etc.) meant to provide expenses for a missionary undertaking. Such missionaries deserved help because they were representatives of Christ himself.

The first missionaries were motivated totally by their consideration of God, having set out for his sake. They accepted nothing from the heathen, not a bit of support or financial help. This probably was done to remove any possibility of suspicion. No one could then suspect that the preacher was seeking his own gain. It may also have been a continuation of the emphasis on separation between that which was of God and that which was against him. The early church seems not to have coveted the devil's wealth.

Some years ago a church-related university was offered a large sum of money by a man who had made his fortune in a business which had been for years considered unworthy of Christians by the churches that supported that university. The school had pressing financial needs, but its administration declined the gift. Another university, also church-related but to a different denomination, was offered the same gift and eagerly accepted. It was commonly said "that money had served the devil long enough." The early church apparently did not share such an attitude. It was to the Lord that those first missionaries turned for help.

Wonderful it was that God's help was ready. It was ready in the person of a man, Gaius, the follower of the truth. John wrote to him to say: "We ought to support such men, that we may be fellow workers in the truth." A large lesson of spiritual truth is contained in that simple statement. Gaius became a missionary through his money. He became a fellow worker with Demetrius and all the others in whose ministry he had invested.

All too frequently God's people do not see beyond the collection plate or the offering box. It requires spiritual insight to follow your money into the lives of God's servants so that you become a fellow worker with the missionary, pastor, and Christian teacher. William Carey, with whom the modern missionary movement began, is remembered for having said to his fellow Baptists that he would venture to go down if they would hold the ropes. God's people today need to get another hand-hold on those ropes. Gaius had a tight grip on that rope.

THOMAS:
WHO EVOKED THE LAST BEATITUDE
JOHN 20:29

The first three Gospels record nothing of Thomas but his name, but John brings that disciple to life for his readers. Although Thomas has been most often called "doubting Thomas," John called him Didymus, the twin. Thomas is the Hebrew word that means "twin," even as Didymus is the Greek word.

In an early apocryphal book called the Acts of Thomas, the identity of this man was further expanded to include the idea that he was the twin brother of Jesus. In that book Thomas is called by the additional name Judas—Judas Thomas or Judas the Twin. In Mark 6:3 and Matthew 13:55 Jesus is said to have had a brother named Judah (or Judas); thus it was thought that Thomas was none other than the twin brother of Jesus (Acts of Thomas 31).

Many fanciful stories came to exist about this disciple who in reality is only known through John's Gospel.

When Jesus was called to Bethany because Lazarus was at the point of death, the reader of John's Gospel gets his first real insight into Thomas. Bethany, where Lazarus lived, was near Jerusalem, and Jesus was already the object of hatred in Jerusalem. The authorities in Jerusalem had determined that Jesus must die. To ask Jesus to return to Bethany was tantamount to asking him to commit suicide Thomas thought. When Jesus indicated his determination to respond to the call of his friends, Thomas expressed both his pessimism and devotion in saying "Let us also go, that we may die with him" (11:16).

When Jesus spoke with his disciples in the upper room after their last meal together, he attempted to prepare them for those terrible events of the morrow when he would be taken from them and crucified. Such was beyond their understanding, but it was Thomas who expressed the perplexity of them all when he said, "We do not know where you go and how can we know the way" (14:1–6). There were many unresolved questions in the mind of Thomas, and he could not be quiet. Jesus told Thomas, "I am the way."

After the death of Jesus, Thomas, wounded in spirit and sore of heart, separated himself from his fellows. There was still much that was unresolved in his mind. When told later by the disciples that Jesus was alive again, the missing saint expressed the doubt for which he has ever been remembered: "Unless I see in his hands the print of the nails, and place my finger in the mark of the nails, and place my hand in his side, I will not believe" (20:25, RSV).

Eight days later it was Thomas, who, having rejoined the disciples, was confronted with the living Christ. He cried out, "My Lord and my God." Life is like that: out of the greatest struggles come the most glorious victories. There can be little doubt that

John intended Thomas' confession, the finest and fullest Christological pronouncement in the Gospel, should be the climax of his book. Against such a setting Jesus pronounced his last beatitude, "Blessed are those who have not seen and yet have believed" (20: 29*b*, RSV).

Some have admired Thomas as an honest doubter. It is true that he did not ask for something the other disciples had not received, to see Jesus for himself! It was not a special revelation that he sought but the same evidence that was given to the others. Christians may be glad this story was given by John because it reveals that the resurrection of Jesus was subjected to the severest tests. It also reveals the forthright and daring recognition with which some of Christ's closest followers questioned that resurrection. No compliment to Thomas, however, can be found there. Thomas was not presented as an ideal but rather as a representative of those who live on a lower plane religiously, those who demand the evidences of the material and physical universe for the acceptance of the gospel.

John's Gospel seems to have been the last of the Gospels to have been written. The years were accumulating, and this last beatitude of Jesus may well have been selected and set in the climax of the Gospel because the author was deeply conscious of many who would never have the opportunity to see, touch, or hear the resurrected Christ. Are not the words of the last beatitude especially needed in a century that to a large degree has rejected everything that does not find its proof in the scientist's laboratory?

Look carefully at the basis for the last beatitude. The blessed of the Lord are those who have believed but who have done this without the evidence of this world in firsthand experience. What did it mean "to believe"? It was Thomas' belief that was commended, it was his "Unless I see . . . I will not believe" that was rebuked. Thomas' belief was revealed in his declaration, "My Lord and my God." The faith of Thomas was much more than satisfaction about the fact of Lazarus' resurrection, but that had not meant much to him spiritually. No, Thomas moved far beyond the fact of Jesus' resurrection to the person of Christ: "My Lord and my God."

Adolpli Deissmann observed that the combination of "Lord and God" was frequently heard at the close of the first century in the worship of Caesar. Suetonius, the Roman historian, wrote that the Emperor Domitian demanded this title, and would not so much as read a letter if it were not addressed to him as "Lord and God." "My Lord" was the favorite designation for Jesus in the early church, by it confession was made of the absolute sovereignty of Jesus and thus also a confession of absolute submission on the part of the confessor. "Lord" in the Greek Old Testament many times equalled "God." Thus Thomas' fuller statement was close at hand; and, as was frequently true in John's language, both the biblical and the Hellenistic use of the day are close together. Jesus in person was actually addressed as "God" in John's Gospel alone. There can be no doubt that the word stood without exception for absolute deity. Thomas not only bowed before Jesus as Lord in submission but also worship before him as God.

Nothing short of the full confession of Thomas can claim the blessing of the resurrected Christ. The Lord's words were not spoken to commend the nebulous concept of faith that is common in the twentieth century, more or less the equivalent of "thinking positively." They were spoken to commend the full acceptance of Jesus as Lord and God.

In what could this last beatitude possibly consist? How could faithful but sightless men be so blessed as Jesus said? Many times Christians of the twentieth century envy those saints of the first century as those possessed of higher spiritual privileges because they saw the Lord in the days of his flesh. It is difficult to really accept the last beatitude, is it not? Could it possibly be true? Yes, there really is a special blessing for those who believe and have not seen! It is true because faith is generated by the Spirit of God within, not by the sight of the eye. The Spirit of God is better than the human eye. Following Thomas' confession, Jesus breathed on the disciples and said, "Receive ye the Holy Ghost." Some commentators have felt that John is in conflict with Acts and the account of Pentecost where the Spirit was given. Some, however, have called this a prelibation of Pentecost—a foretaste—that the apostles might know how rich was the vintage waiting for them. There is an inward state of heart due to the Holy Spirit's working within that makes gospel truth believable the moment it is declared. F. W. Robertson wrote: "Love is credible to a loving heart: purity is credible to a pure mind. Of course, that inward state could not *reveal* a fact like the resurrection; but it can *receive* the fact the moment it is revealed without requiring evidence." What a blessing the Holy Spirit is within men to convict them of sin and righteousness and judgment!

Christians of the twentieth century also have the book. In fact, they have sometimes been referred to as "people of the book." Now bibliolatry, worship of the Bible, is not worthy of Christians, but could there be a Christian worthy of his name who did not cherish that book, the Bible? Who could begin to total up the blessings found in that book of books? Remember that the very next words to follow the last beatitude are these: "Now Jesus did many other signs in the presence of the disciples, which are not written in this book; but these are written that you may believe that Jesus is the Christ, the Son of God, and that believing you may have life in his name." In what sense is the Bible the word of God to men?

It is God's word in that it is a true record of the deeds of God, and the Christ-event is the climatic act of God. It is also the word of God in that within its revelation there is the power to create spiritual experience. What a blessing the word of God is that men might believe and have life in Christ's name.

The last beatitude is a reminder that God cares for the people of the twentieth century as well as those of the first. The people of this day are not even an afterthought in the plan of God. From the beginning, God's blessing was laid up for modern man. "Blessed are those who have not seen and yet believe." Those words are pure grace!

A speaker in a chapel service told poignantly of standing in the hospital with a lovely couple to whom a child had been recently born. To the unspeakable sorrow of the parents, the doctors had verified the first fears that this baby would never see nor hear. The speaker said that he felt he stood in the presence of divine love as the mother, holding the little blanket-swathed bundle, said through her tears: "My precious little one, though you will never see me nor hear my voice, I give you my life that you may never wonder if I love you." It is something like that for men today because the Savior says to men of faith, "I give you my life that you may never wonder if I love you." "Blessed are those who have not seen and yet believe."

TIMOTHY:
PAUL'S "P.K."
1 TIMOTHY 1:2

What is it that makes the preacher's kid so mean?" the tired old question asks. The answer seems never to have mustered the humor for which it was intended "Playing with the deacons' kids." Such words were designed no doubt to serve as a reminder that the preacher's child is human and subject to the same weaknesses as all others. They also suggest that people always seem to expect more of the minister's family and are more critical of them.

Timothy was in a sense Paul's "P. K." His home was at Lystra, and his natural family was racially mixed. His father had been a Greek, and the tense of the verb used in the record of Acts has suggested to some that his father was already dead. At least his father never entered the story. Eunice, Timothy's mother, was a

Jewess, and along with her mother, Lois, had likely been among Paul's converts at Lystra when he first preached there. Though Timothy was quite young, he too was already a disciple, being converted, no doubt, by Paul since he was later addressed by the apostle as "my true child in the faith" (1 Tim. 1:2).

Paul was old enough to have been Timothy's father. The younger man may have been only fourteen or fifteen years of age when Paul came that second time to Lystra. There was a place for a young helper like Timothy in the missionary party. Though only a boy, Timothy was much appreciated by the church at Lystra and even at Iconium.

Timothy seemed to the older preacher to be just the helper he needed. Timothy had a background that Paul could deeply appreciate. When later Paul wrote of Timothy's heritage, he said that from childhood Timothy had known the Scriptures (see 2 Tim. 2:15). A. T. Robertson suggested that Paul in that remark was echoing his own experience in his home at Tarsus. No doubt also Paul could sense as an older preacher the promise of tomorrow in the life of the younger man whom he invited to join the missionary party. It seems that from the very beginning Paul assumed the role of a father to young Timothy.

Standing in the place of a father in Israel, Paul required the circumcision of Timothy before allowing him to participate in the mission enterprise. It was strange that Paul who was such an opponent of the circumcision party (those who taught the necessity of a Christian's keeping the law of Moses) would require circumcision for anyone, but Timothy was that one. Some have felt that Paul's attitude about the circumcision of Timothy indicates that the event took place before the writing of Galatians in which he criticized the circumcision party most severely.

Paul's problem was a practical one. Timothy belonged to no one.

For Jews Timothy would have been counted as a Gentile because he was the uncircumcised son of a Greek, even though ordinarily Jewishness was established through the mother. To the Gentiles, however, Timothy was a Jew. His mother was a Jewess, and the boy had been brought up in her religion. By having Timothy circumcised, Paul made Timothy legitimate for Jews. Practical necessity for the effectiveness of the young man in the gospel ministry was the only real issue. Paul and Silas then took Timothy with them. He seems to have been commissioned and commended to the ministry of the gospel by the elders of the church at Lystra, with Paul presiding. Timothy was Paul's son in the ministry as well as his child in faith.

People have always expected much of the preacher's child, and it was none the less true of Timothy who was closely associated with Paul. Perhaps anyone else's failure would have gone almost unnoticed, but not the failures of a young man so closely associated with the mighty apostle.

Failures there seem to have been. For instance there was the Corinthian situation. What troubles Paul had at Corinth! That situation always needed attention. Often Paul expressed his own frustration with the Corinthian church. In the course of his many dealings with that church Paul sent Timothy, perhaps then just past twenty years of age, to be his spokesman. Paul's opposition seems literally to have "cleaned that young man's plow." In writing to the church Paul was at special pains to support Timothy: "When Timothy comes, see that you put him at ease among you, for he is doing the work of the Lord, as I am. So let no one despise him" (1 Cor. 16:10 f., RSV). Things didn't go any better, however, at Corinth, and Paul's second letter to that church indicates that he had to put matters in other hands than Timothy's.

Some question the genuineness of the pastoral epistles, but that is not at issue here. Two of those letters were addressed by Paul to Timothy. The years had passed, and Timothy still needed to be encouraged. Perhaps at the time of the pastorals Timothy was just past thirty years of age and confronted with many problems in his Christian service. Paul was especially plain in declaring: "Let no one despise your youth, but set the believers an example in speech and conduct, in love, in faith, in purity" (1 Tim. 4:12, RSV).

The conditions which Paul foresaw years before when he said farewell to the Ephesian elders had materialized (Acts 20:29 ff.). Some men were preaching a different doctrine, given to fables and endless genealogies, seemingly an incipient Jewish gnosticism. The results of that false preaching were disputes, violent argumentation, and a great emptiness of real spiritual truth. Timothy seems at the time to have been acting as a traveling evangelist, and Paul wrote to urge him to remain at Ephesus in order to deal with that barren philosophizing which was threatening to destroy the church. What a formidable responsibility was laid upon the young preacher. Paul seems never to have lost his confidence in Timothy and always wrote to him in a tone of deepest sympathy, something that Paul seems to have had difficulty in expressing for others, such as John Mark. No doubt the close bond between Paul and Timothy made the difference.

Paul's last word was for Timothy, and how appropriate that it should have been so. Second Timothy, written from Paul's last imprisonment, was especially a word to encourage his "beloved child" to be worthy of his heritage of faith. Paul begged the younger man to kindle into a blaze the gift of God that was in him (2 Tim. 1:6), to be courageous and strong for the service of Christ. The last chapter of Paul's last letter is weighted with concern for Timothy. He was admonished to preach the word (4:2) and to endure suffering (4:5). With a concern that is felt in the very reading of the words, Paul said, "fulfil your ministry" (4:5*c*). Who could fail to sense the pathos in the appeal, "Do your best to come to me soon" (4:9)?

Many an older man has been as a father to a younger man in the service of Christ, but strangely the record of prominent men in such a role is not notable. Perhaps important men live under such pressures of life that they just do not have time to cultivate the younger men who answer God's call. Paul was different in that his career was distinguished by the many young men whom he inspired and developed into effective servants of Christ, and Timothy, as far as the apostle's affection was concerned, was in the forefront of them all.

I know a man in Christ who, as a boy, years ago had as pastor the famous George W. Truett. When that boy was in Baylor University, his beloved teacher was the saintly (yes, that is the correct word) J. B. Tidwell, professor of Bible for many years there. That boy loved both of those men immensely and knew their love in return. That boy, turned man, will always remember a day in the fall of 1941 when he was called to the telephone in old Brooks Hall. It was the beloved pastor's voice saying that he was on campus for a meeting of the trustees and asking if that boy could come to Dr. Tidwell's office for a few minutes of fellowship. What an hour that was. Those two old men on their knees in prayer throughout what remained of a winter afternoon. The heat was off in the building, and both men were bundled in their overcoats against the cold. When all had been said, Dr. Truett couldn't get up. That boy will never forget the sight of the tear-stained pastor's face as it passed before his when he hauled that dear man to his feet from the experience of prayer. That man I know will forever be blest by the memory of those two saints who loved him as a boy. Timothy was like that for he was Paul's true child.

PHILIP:
THE "TRY HIM, YOU'LL LIKE HIM" SAINT
JOHN 1:43

Try it, you'll like it!" the radio blared its insistent demand. How like the twentieth century to judge everything in the realm of experience. "Try it, you'll like it" challenges modern man a thousand times or more in connection with a thousand or more items every day. "Try it, you'll like it" rests the verdict squarely on experience.

Philip, the apostle, was that kind of man. He would have felt very comfortable in the modern world. He understood and was sympathetic to the verdict of experience. He wasn't much on theology, nor was reasoning his long suit. He was tops, however, when it came to making a judgment on what could be known by experience. Many today would call him a practical man.

Philip was the first man Jesus called to be a follower. He was one of those earnest Jews who, along with Andrew and others, had repented under the preaching of John the Baptist. He too had opened his heart to the hope, almost too big to hold, that the longed-for Messiah was actually coming in that day. Andrew and his unnamed companion were the first of John's disciples to follow Jesus, but Philip was the first that Jesus called.

Was Philip in the crowd that day when John the Baptist pointed to Jesus, saying, "Behold, the Lamb of God?" If he was there, why didn't he follow Jesus as Andrew did? There seems to be a story in the statement that Jesus found Philip. There are references in the Scriptures that are "a sermon in a word." This may be one of them. Even as John later wrote that Jesus "had to pass through Samaria," with much significance attached to that necessity; so with Philip it was written, "the next day Jesus decided to go to Galilee, and he found Philip and said to him, 'Follow me.' " Jesus was looking for Philip that day. He was prepared to meet Philip on his own terms, allowing him to see for himself.

By actual count Jesus laid his claim across the lives of men with the words "follow me" more often than with any others, but Philip was the first man to hear them from his lips. Those words were a call to decision, but they were also words that invited the validation of his claims by the experience of shared life.

Those first disciples were men unable to keep from sharing their newfound faith in Jesus. Even as Andrew had gone for Simon, his brother, so Philip went for Nathanael, his friend. Nathanael was anything but receptive to the witness of Philip. No doubt Philip was no match for Nathanael in a theological debate, and Nathanael had sufficient reasons for doubting that the Messiah could possibly be from Nazareth. How was such a situation to be met? It was natural to Philip to answer, "Come and see." "Try him, you'll like him" was the essence of Philip's approach to Nathanael.

Philip was the calculating disciple. It was of Philip that Jesus inquired concerning the feeding of the five thousand. Because Jesus turned to Philip with this problem, some have thought that this disciple was in charge of their commissary and might even have been the cook for the disciple band. Also, because Philip so quickly replied that it would require two hundred denarii just to give a bit to each person in that huge crowd, some have thought that he was already calculating the practical requirements of feeding such a large group. Philip did have a mind like that.

Did those Greeks who wanted to see Jesus come to Philip because he was the most open of the disciples (John 12:20-22)? Philip was not prepared to deal with such a request himself, but he did act on it. He took it to Andrew. Philip might be uncertain as to how far to go himself, or what exactly needed to be done, but he couldn't live with inaction.

In those last hours Jesus shared with his disciples just preceding his betrayal, arrest, and execution, he sought to interpret those coming events for his disciples. He spoke the memorable words about his Father's house and going to prepare a place for them. Thomas was the first to express inability to understand, saying: "Lord, we do not know where you are going; how can we know the way." To this Jesus replied, "If you had known me, you would have known my Father also; henceforth you know him and have seen him." Now that was something Philip felt that he, of all people, should be able to validate. If any disciple knew what he had seen, Philip did, but it was impossible to follow Jesus' meaning. Therefore, Philip entered the discussion with his insistent: "Lord, show us the Father and we shall be satisfied."

How like modern men Philip was. He wanted to see. No doubt he had in mind something like an Old Testament theophany when he said, "Show us the Father," some appearance of God such as Moses or Isaiah had known, a convincing vision of God. All of today's discoveries and inventions, modern science in the whole, are based on the human senses. What can be seen and handled can be accepted and trusted. There isn't much room for any other evidence for the mind of modern man.

To empirically minded Philip Jesus spoke perhaps the most daring words he ever uttered: "Have I been with you so long, and yet you do not know me, Philip? He who has seen me has seen the Father; how can you say, 'Show us the Father'? " Surely Jesus didn't appear much, if any, different from other men, just to look at him. What was it that Jesus expected Philip should have seen because they had shared life together? Jesus had not concealed his inner life from his disciples. Philip should have seen God because of Jesus' life. No temptation caused Jesus' fall; he was altogether pure. Jesus had loved men with a divine love, even sinful men. Jesus had lifted men and remade their lives as only God could do. He had brought men out, before the very eyes of those disciples, into the liberty and glory of sons of God. He worked with a divine power, healing the sick, raising the dead, exercising the very control of nature itself. To all of this the disciples had been witnesses. They had seen God. Jesus recognized the validity of the kind of evidence that Philip asked. He insisted, however, that it had been already given.

Occasionally, some student who has been under the ministry of an effective preacher whom he genuinely respects will capture something in himself of his hero, not the cheap imitation of voice or manner, but something of the spirit of the man himself. Students of A. B. Bruce, the saintly expositor of Scripture, often said that they had seen in their teacher the glory of God. A great teacher often stamps his students with something of himself. Arthur John

Gossip tells a story of one of A. B. Bruce's students, W. M. Macgregor, a most successful pastor in his day. Churchmen of that day were astounded when they heard that Macgregor was giving up his important pulpit for a professorship. When asked about his decision, the famous pastor replied with modesty that he had learned from his beloved teacher Bruce that which he felt he must pass on.

More than any mortal catches the spirit and reproduces the life of another man, Jesus possessed the life of God. To Philip particularly, and in response to his inquiry, Jesus said: "Truly, truly, I say to you, he who believes in me will also do the works that I do; and greater works than these will he do." There will be a real bequest of life and power to the one who believes on Jesus. Philip's premise will be proved worthy all over again: "Try him, you'll like him!" Pass it on!

ZACCHAEUS:
THE LITTLE MAN WHO GREW
LUKE 19:1-10

Zacchaeus—how clearly he can be seen in one's mind as he climbed a sycamore tree to see Jesus. Zacchaeus was a small man; he was too short to see over the crowd. So he climbed a tree to see Jesus as he passed through Jericho on his way to Jerusalem.

Was it curiosity only that took Zacchaeus up that tree to see an important person who was passing by? Did Luke mean something more when he explained that climb with the words "to see who he was?" From subsequent events it would seem likely that there was something more. The instantaneous response to Jesus, the fulness of his dedication, would suggest that this rich but lonely, proud but snubbed, successful but unfulfilled man was seeking something more from life the day he made his famous climb.

Jericho was a very great city, and Zacchaeus was a very important man there. The city was situated on a major travel route. It was also in an immensely fertile district famous for its date palms and known around the civilized earth for its balsam groves. It was a district which Josephus described as "the fattest in Palestine." To be the chief publican, or tax collector, such a place offered all kinds of opportunities for a clever man to feather his own nest. Zacchaeus made the most of everyone of them. Small wonder that such a man who had sold out to the Roman conquerors was ostracised by his own people. To the Jews, he was a moral, religious, and social outcast.

How did Jesus know Zacchaeus? Some have suggested that the little man, jostled rather unkindly by his neighbors who would not make room for the despised tax collector, was jeered by those who had prevented his seeing Jesus. Perhaps they shouted his name in ridicule as he unceremoniously climbed that tree.

There is also an old tradition which may be only the product of a vivid imagination, but it notes that Jesus had a close follower who had once been a tax collector like Zacchaeus, Matthew. The story has it that Matthew and Zacchaeus had been friends and that Jesus had been especially alerted to watch for him.

Most likely, Luke understood that Jesus in ways that belonged only to him because of who he was knew both Zacchaeus and his condition. It was truly a divinely appointed meeting that day toward which the chief publican unknowingly moved when he climbed to his perch in the sycamore tree. Jesus was on his way to Jerusalem to die. This was his last visit to Jericho, and Zacchaeus was one of the last men of record that Jesus called to himself during his earthly ministry.

As far as the record goes, Jesus never invited himself to be a guest in any home except that of Zacchaeus. The people of Jericho couldn't believe there could be much to Jesus if he would go home with such a man as the publican. They were quite certain that no real prophet would have had anything to do with a man like Zacchaeus. For Luke, however, Jesus' interest in the chief publican of Jericho, his compassion for a man described as lost, was supremely important evidence that he was the Messiah.

"Lost" is a term of special importance in the Gospel of Luke. To remember the fifteenth chapter of Luke is to recall a lost sheep, a lost coin, and two lost boys. Luke would have his readers remember above all else that to be lost means to have wandered away from God, to be separated from God. It does not mean, however, that God no longer loves that lost man. Zacchaeus is an example of what it means to be lost. Conversely, to be saved means to be found, so it is that Jesus seeks the lost. Through Jesus, God makes his effort to reclaim the individual, to bring him back, as he did Zacchaeus.

Someone suggested that Zacchaeus was so ready for Jesus that he was converted before he hit the ground. There must have been a marvellous kindness in Jesus' approach to him; and the publican was, no doubt, a man who knew how to make decisions. When that decision came may be debated, but that salvation came cannot be. Jesus himself said, "Today salvation has come to this house." The evidence of salvation has always been a changed man, and Zacchaeus gave great evidence of such a change. It is small wonder that he remembered things in the past that needed to be made right; salvation is like that. It was wonderful, however, that he said: "Behold, Lord, the half of my goods I give to the poor; and if I have defrauded any one of anything, I restore it fourfold." As the old country preacher said: "When the pocketbook gets baptized, it is a good sign of a genuine experience." The law of Moses said that in the case of robbery, if the stolen goods could not themselves be returned, double the value was to be repaid (Ex. 22:4,7). If, instead of being caught, the thief voluntarily confessed and offered restitution, only one-fifth was added to the value of the goods (Lev. 6:5; Num. 5:7). What Zacchaeus decided to do was far beyond any requirement of the law; it was his standing tall in the gospel.

There was once a grandmother who regularly measured and marked behind the kitchen door the height of each of her grandchildren, carefully noting for each his name and the date. As the years passed, the room was often repainted, but never that spot behind the door. There came a day for each child when the measurements were no longer made. Grown, away at college, off to the war, the grandchildren had made their last mark behind that grandmother's door. While growing up, each advance in height was proudly noted. The only real sadness came when one of the boys, wanting very much to reach the magic six-foot level, stopped growing short of his goal. Paul remarked one day that Christians are people who are growing up in Jesus.

Zacchaeus' name meant "pure," but he had been anything but that. Jesus called him "a son of Abraham," meaning no doubt that he was a true heir of the covenant that God had made with the patriarch. Out of his experience with the chief publican, Jesus uttered the immortal words that caught up the whole meaning of his life and ministry: "The Son of man came to seek and to save the lost." Today the words might be expressed this way: "A man never stands taller than when he bows his life to Jesus." Zacchaeus was a man who really grew that day when Jesus came to Jericho.

ANDREW:
THE FISHERMAN'S SAINT
JOHN 1:40

There was a neighbor once who had a saint for everything. One protected him while he drove his automobile. Another helped him locate the things that he had lost or misplaced. Yet another guarded his home while he was away. He literally had a saint for everything. Now evangelicals have never taken kindly to that conception of saints, with one exception. Andrew is the "patron saint" for evangelicals who are fishers of men.

A church in the large city had many military persons in the worship services during those days of war. One young sailor, out of lonliness and curiosity, noticed the announcement that on Sunday afternoon the Andrew Band would meet and visitors would be cordially welcomed. Imagine his surprise when he discovered the gathering was for the purpose of learning how to bring men to Christ.

Andrew, one of the first two men to follow Jesus, was the first man of record to bring anyone to the Savior. Andrew, who came from the town of Bethsaida on the Sea of Galilee, was a fisherman. He understood well the language Jesus used that day when he spoke to Simon Peter: "henceforth you will be catching men" (Luke 5:10*b*, RSV). Yes, if there is any evangelical saint, it must be Andrew who has inspired many to seek to bring others to the Savior.

Andrew had been a follower and disciple of John the Baptist. No doubt he was one of John's most sincere and earnest listeners. Under the preaching of the mighty prophet, Andrew had repented and opened his heart to God, earnestly looking for the arrival of the messianic age which John professed to be announcing. Prepared in his own heart to receive the Messiah when he came and remaining close at hand to John who was to identify the Christ, Andrew must have felt a thrill run through his flesh the day the Baptist pointed out Jesus and said, "Behold, the Lamb of God." Along with an unnamed companion, probably Zebedee's young son, John, Andrew hastened to follow Jesus. Andrew is really only known on the pages of Scripture through those incidents which John recorded. Their names are linked in many traditions. What a day those two must have spent with Jesus, two men who would never be the same again.

The next day the first thing that Andrew did was to share his new found faith with another, his own brother Simon. Andrew told Simon, "We have found the Messiah" (John 1:41, RSV). How direct! How full! How personal! How earnest! How adequate! Thus it was that Simon came to Jesus.

Jesus looked at Andrew's brother and said: "So you are Simon the son of John? You shall be called Cephas (which means Peter)." For the first and last time Simon was to be recognized as Andrew's brother. From that time forward, Andrew was always to be "Simon's brother." Everyone knows the importance of Simon Peter in the Christian community; but Andrew, who was willing to take the lesser place, should not be forgotten. There was never a hint of jealousy or envy on Andrew's part because of the position of his brother, and not all the disciples were free from such feelings. What a matchless day's work Andrew did when he brought his brother, Simon, to Jesus.

Who could call the name of Alypius, the friend of Aurelius Augustinus, to whom that distracted young man turned in the hour of his spiritual need and in whose garden he sat when God spoke to bring salvation? Many people now however, know the name of Augustine, the theologian. Could anyone call the name of the man who, on the evening of May 24, 1738, influenced a very unwilling John Wesley to attend the prayer meeting in Aldersgate Street? Wesley later said he felt his sins had been taken away at that time. Could anyone call the name of Edward Kimball, successful merchant in Boston, who, seeing the young D. L. Moody at his task of selling shoes, insisted that the country boy go with him to his Sunday School which led to Moody's conversion? Life seems to have the habit of using so-called "little" people to bring those to Christ who become "outstanding" in his service.

There was a day also when Andrew set the stage for one of the two miracles of Jesus mentioned in all four of the Gospels. It was Andrew who rose to the bait when Jesus asked about the possibility of feeding the vast multitude of five thousand who had followed him into the country to hear him preach. It was Andrew who knew about the boy with his lunch, five barley loaves and two small fish. It was a typical boy's lunch, cheap bread and two sardine-like fish.

One wonders why Andrew even bothered to bring that boy to Jesus, but he did. Andrew was always bringing somebody to Jesus. He understood that to be his task; the rest was up to Jesus. From such a little lunch the multitude was fed, with twelve basketfuls left over. Jesus did the rest!

Andrew's name was really Greek, though not uncommon among Jews. John tells that in the last days of Jesus' earthly ministry certain Greeks expressed a desire to see Jesus. Some have thought it significant that those Greeks made their approach to the only other disciple beside Andrew to have a Greek name, Philip. Why didn't Philip just take them to Jesus? Did he wonder about the propriety of Greeks being with Jesus? Perhaps he feared that the presence of those Gentiles with Jesus would just anger the Jewish opposition all the more? No one can say why, but Philip obviously hesitated to take the Greeks to Jesus. The best Philip could do was talk over the problem with Andrew. It was Andrew who made the difference. They went and told Jesus. Andrew was certain that was the way to answer men who said: "Sir, we wish to see Jesus."

A story has been told almost from the beginning of the Reformation about Martin Luther as a boy. According to the story Martin as a boy went to school to an old German teacher who had a stange practice. As he entered his classroom each morning, he removed his hat and bowed to the boys in his class. When someone questioned him about that unprecedented habit, he answered that the teacher never knew what any of his students might someday become. Martin Luther certainly justified the old teacher's reverence for the student's potential. Who knows what any man will become when he is brought to Jesus?

Andrew was the disciple who was always reverent before the spiritual potential of men. With a fisherman's excitement for the unknown (one never knows what he is about to pull out), he cast the net again and again, always hoping to catch someone for Jesus.

ONESIMUS:
THE RUNAWAY SAINT
PHILEMON

The ringing of the telephone in the middle of the night awakened nearly everyone in the house. Such calls were not unknown in the preacher's home, and they nearly always signaled trouble. The boyish voice of the speaker reminded the preacher of a week at Glorieta Baptist Assembly. The preacher had met a boy from the distant city who had come along almost as an extra. He wasn't a member of the church that sponsored his group, indeed he was not a Christian. The preacher and the boy came to know each other through the Bible study class they shared. Many long conversations during the afternoons of that week helped the preacher know a lonely boy, at odds with the world, estranged from his family, and groping to find his way into life. Many conversations also helped the boy know the Savior with all the promise and hope bound up in Christianity. It had been a tender moment when that boy had said yes to Jesus. Now he was calling, having just arrived in town with no place to stay.

The boy had run away from home; at least his parents did not know where he was. He poured out the frustration of his soul, telling about the impossibility of getting through to his parents who had never accepted his new religion. Problems were many and serious, but step by step the situation was faced. A call was made to the parents to calm their fears, and at last that boy was persuaded to board a bus for home. Mixed emotions swept through the preacher's heart as he watched the boy who didn't want to go home board that bus.

What did Paul feel that day when he watched Onesimus start back to Colossae and back to slavery? What ran through the mind of Onesimus, the runaway slave, as he started back to his master? The circumstances surrounding this strange scene were almost unbelievable. Onesimus was a slave, belonging either to Philemon or Archippus his son. Onesimus had not only run away but had also stolen from his master. How he had managed to get from Colossae in Asia to Rome is not told, the runaway had met Paul, the prisoner at Rome. Paul led Onesimus to faith in Christ and became so attached to this new convert that he spoke of feeling for him as a father would for his child (Philem. 10). In sending him back, Paul evidenced that he felt as if he were sending his own heart and expressed the wish that he might have kept him.

Philemon, the former master, was also Paul's friend and apparently his convert too. In sending the slave back, the apostle gently reminded the master that he owed Paul a debt in the Spirit and suggested that he discharge that obligation by receiving his slave back as a brother, which may have meant to set him free. All this was written in the letter called Philemon which was carried, along with Colossians, by Onesimus and Paul's helper Tychicus to its destination. What a confidence Paul manifested in the power of the gospel. He believed it could cause a master to forgive and free a runaway slave who had robbed him. He believed that a runaway slave could be trusted to return to his former master and live before him the life of a Christian witness, even if it should mean unrelieved servitude.

Ignatius of Antioch mentioned in a letter addressed to the church at Ephesus the beloved and faithful bishop of that church, and his name was Onesimus. He pled with the people there to live worthily of the gospel because they had such a faithful bishop. "Onesimus" means useful, and Paul, writing to Philemon, made a play on the meaning of the slave's name by saying: "Formerly he was useless to you, but now he is indeed useful to you and to me." (Philem. 11, RSV). Ignatius in his letter to Ephesus made exactly the same play on the meaning of the bishop's name. Since the name was also common for slaves but shunned by free men, the bishop of whom Ignatius wrote might well have been the slave Paul sent home. Since Ignatius' letter was written about A.D. 115, Onesimus would have been only a boy when he ran away to Rome, and a man in his seventies when Ignatius wrote to Ephesus.

An ancient tradition indicated that the New Testament began first to be assembled by the church at Ephesus under the auspices of its bishop. The first parts of the New Testament to be joined were the letters of Paul which were collected there in Ephesus. Could it be that, humanly speaking, the reason the short, personal letter to Philemon was preserved to be included in the New Testament when other letters addressed to entire churches did not survive was because the bishop at Ephesus was Onesimus, the runaway slave who became a saint?

THE SAINTS GO MARCHING BY

ROMANS 16

What a conglomeration of saints there was in Rome! Or at least it seems they, twenty-four of them plus the groups described but not named, were at Rome, because they are listed and greeted in the last chapter of Romans. Paul had not at that time been to Rome, and some have wondered how he could have greeted such a large number by name at a place where he had never been. Some of them, such as Priscilla and Aquila, would ordinarily be associated with Ephesus at the time Paul wrote Romans. Paul ministered longer at Ephesus than at most places and knew many people quite well there, although some of that ministry at Ephesus was yet in the future at the time Romans was written. Also, Romans seems to come to its natural close at 15:33. Because of all of this, many have thought that Romans 16 must have been a fragment of a letter that was originally written to the church at Ephesus but got tacked on to the end of Romans.

There is no manuscript evidence that Romans was ever circulated without chapter sixteen. Rome was the capital of the world; all roads led to Rome. Travelers from all over the world went to Rome. Once it had been been the home of Priscilla and Aquila, who might well have returned there. No doubt people from Rome went abroad, and no doubt some of them, even as Priscilla and Aquila, had met Paul while they were away from Rome. The people mentioned seem likely, then, to have been people of the Roman church.

The church is really the people. Sometimes that is difficult to remember. People speak of the church's meeting place as the church. Sometimes a denominational structure is called a church; but really a church is people. Much can be learned about the early church at Rome from the people who gave it existence!

From the personal greeting, it is observed that there were several women among the believers in Rome. Remembering the restrictions placed upon women generally in the first century, and especially by the Jews in religious matters, it is remarkable that this many women were called forth from the Roman church for tender greetings. Those who have accused Paul of less than an appreciative attitude toward women should note Paul's friends at Rome who were women, especially the unnamed mother of Rufus of whom Paul wrote "also his mother and mine." From the days of Jesus' earthly ministry, women rendered meaningful service and were tenderly regarded for that fact. In the New Testament women really come into their spiritual liberation.

Racial differences were also represented in the church at Rome. Some of the names in Romans 16 are obviously Latin and probably represent people of that extraction: Julia, Urbanus, Tryphaena, and so forth. Still other names are Greek and probably represent people who were from that background: Persis, Asyncritus, Stachys, Hermes, and others. Others mentioned, though bearing Greek or Latin names (or the Latin of Hebrew names), were undoubtedly Jewish: Prisca, Aquila, Mary, Herodion, and others. Obviously, the early church was a spiritual melting pot in which differences of race and culture were sublimated to the overpowering reality of Christian fellowship. The Jew might hate the Roman. The Roman might lord it over the world. The Greek might look down on both, but in the Lord and his church, all that was swept away. They were one in the Lord.

Sanday and Headlam have shown that a large number of the names in this list have been found in inscriptions taken from the ruins of ancient Rome. Many were undoubtedly names commonly borne by slaves. Paul greeted those who belonged to the family (household) of Aristobulus. Also, he greeted those of the family (household) of Narcissus. Now among the Romans, "family" did not describe just those who were kin to a person but to all of his dependants, including slaves. Herod the Great had a grandson named Aristobulus who had long lived at Rome. It may be that some of these had been his slaves. The most famous person of the first century to be named Narcissus was a freedman who was close to the Emperor Claudius, serving as his minister of petitions. These may well have been the slaves of that famous man, indicating that the gospel had penetrated even into the imperial household. Paul later indicated this was true of the emperor's personal guard (Phil. 1:13).

Ampliatus was a common name for a slave. In the oldest of the catacombs in Rome there is a tomb with the name Ampliatus carved in large letters. A Roman would have had three names (nomen, praenomen, cognomen) but a slave only one. Was this Ampliatus a slave, yet buried with distinction by his fellow believers? The early church certainly disregarded the differences in social status that were of utmost importance in the world, and Ampliatus, though a slave, in all probability was held in highest esteem by his brethren.

Among those with Paul at Corinth, from which he wrote Romans, were some men of wealth and influence. Gaius was sufficiently well provided that he could be host to Paul and the entire church as well. Erastus was a prominent man who served as treasurer of the huge and important city of Corinth. In the church there was a leveling of all social distinctions in Christian brotherhood.

Some of the names of the saints in Rome are grouped in such a way as to give the impression that they were associated with some particular gathering of the believers in the vast city of Rome. The homes of the people were of vital significance to the worship of the church. Public buildings were not available and many, such as slaves, had no place to call their own. Paul greeted the church that met in the house of Prisca and Aquila. Two other such gatherings of the church in homes are probably indicated by the words "Greet Asyncritus, Phlegon, Hermes, Patrobas, Hermas and the brethren who are with them" and by the words "Greet Philologus, Julia, Nereus and his sister, and Olympas and all the saints who are with them." Whichever believer could provide room for part of the church to assemble did so, and the small group prayer meetings and worship services oriented to the home were the mainstay of the church in Rome.

Paul also excites the reader's imagination by reference to three members of the church at Rome and three members of the church at Corinth as kinsmen. Because there were so many of this description, some have thought Paul meant simply his fellow Jews, kinsmen according to the flesh, as he speaks of them in Romans 9:3,4. Others think that Paul meant simply to indicate those with whom he had especially close ties of Christian fellowship, as he had so written of Rufus' mother as his own also. Most likely, however, Paul really meant his relatives. Some he describes as having been in Christ before him, which must have meant that they were Christians before he was. Perhaps one of them was Paul's nephew whom the book of Acts indicates came to Paul in the prison at Jerusalem, bringing word of the plot against the apostle's life (Acts 23:12-24).

Some of the Roman church were singled out for special recognition. Epaenetus who was the first in Asia to receive Christ had evidently come to Rome. Ampliatus and Stachys were greeted as "my beloved" in the Lord. Discreetly Paul changed to simply "the beloved" when greeting the woman, Persis. Some, such as Persis, are remembered as having labored in the Lord, giving of themselves unreservedly in the service of Christ, and are appreciated for that fact.

Rufus, who was described as eminent (chosen) in the Lord, is one of the most interesting of all the gathering of those saints at Rome. In the Gospel of Mark, it is noted that Simon of Cyrene, who was compelled to carry Jesus' cross to Golgotha, was the father of two sons, Alexander and Rufus (15:21). Since Mark probably wrote his Gospel for the church at Rome, many have believed Rufus mentioned in Romans to have been Simon's son mentioned by the Evangelist.

Paul admonished the saints at Rome to greet one another with a saintly kiss. Now a kiss in the first century was the common expression of friendship as a public greeting, very much like shaking hands is today. Among Christians, however, it took on a much higher meaning, being associated with the loftiest expression of love in the early church, the observance of the Lord's Supper. In connection with that most holy event, the men in turn kissed one another, beginning from the presiding elder and being passed from one to another as a symbol of their common membership in the family of God. Information from the third century indicates that the women also practiced this act of Christian love, but only with women.

The saintly kiss, then, was the approved greeting for saintly people. One who was not a saint could not give the saintly kiss. Neither could the Christian who promoted divisions in the fellowship or who was in some other way the author of evil pass along the saintly kiss. The saintly kiss was the supreme emblem of those who were one in the Lord Jesus.